To Steve, for everything you've taught,
shared, and given

Share Better
and Stress Less

Share Better and Stress Less

A Guide to Thinking Ecologically about Social Media

Whitney Phillips and Ryan Milner

The MIT Press, the ☰**MiTeen**Press colophon, and MITeen Press
are trademarks of The MIT Press, a department of the
Massachusetts Institute of Technology, and used under license
from The MIT Press. The colophon and MITeen are registered in
the US Patent and Trademark Office.

First edition 2023

Library of Congress Catalog Card Number 2022908681
ISBN 978-1-5362-2874-8

22 23 24 25 26 27 APS 10 9 8 7 6 5 4 3 2 1

Printed in Humen, Dongguan, China

This book was typeset in Archer.

MITeen Press
an imprint of Candlewick Press
99 Dover Street
Somerville, Massachusetts 02144

miteenpress.com
candlewick.com

Contents

Ecological Thinking and You

WHITNEY: There we were, exploring a place we'll call Redwood Adventure Park, a nature attraction in Northern California. It was 2003, and my parents and teenage brother and sister were visiting during my first year of college. We'd decided to drive along the coast and visit every Highway 101 pit stop we could find. Road sign after road sign pointed us to this particular adventure, so five twenty-dollar tickets later, we were in weird redwood heaven. Wooden placards gave background stories on all the trees, and there were carved stumps—of woodland creatures, loggers, and Bigfoot—everywhere. A few months earlier, I'd given myself a buzz cut and dyed my naturally blondish hair black for "I'll show you, world" reasons. It had grown out into an unruly mullet and was flopping around mop-like as I scampered among the living and carved-up trees, giggling at what could only be described as forest clickbait.

After wandering the park's crisscrossing trails, we decided to head over to the forest ridge lookout for a bird's-eye view of the canopy. At the top of a seemingly endless flight of stairs, a worker wearing head-to-toe pink camouflage ushered us onto the viewing platform, gestured around dramatically, and told us in a hushed voice that on one side we'd see the ocean and on the other, "the Awesomeness," which I think just meant more trees.

But before we could climb to the top, my sister needed to finish drinking her hot chocolate. "'Kay, ready," she said when she was finished. She handed her empty cup to my mom, who held it for a moment. Then, looking right at my sister, my mom threw the cup smack on the ground. We all paused. Gasped! Why would she do such a thing? And then my mom started laughing. She bent down to pick up the cup. "The look on your faces!" she said, still laughing. We all started laughing too, and then, of course, as soon as we saw a trash can, she threw the cup away.

This was funny because, for one thing, it was so unexpected. I'd never seen my mom litter in my whole life. It was also funny because it was exactly what you're not supposed to do at a park. If you did, you'd have to walk around in your own mess. Other people would have to walk around in it too, and some of them might get the idea that *hey, fun, it's fine to throw trash here,* making it more likely that more people would throw their trash wherever. From there, it could end up in a river or be swallowed by a goose. The moral of the story, said in my best judgmental Bigfoot voice, is that throwing your trash on the ground when you're at a park doesn't just impact you. It impacts others as well, Mom.

RYAN: Trash, or at least stuff you don't want to have to walk through, is a theme in this book. But instead of actual dirty cups on the ground, we're focused on **information pollution**.

Here's an example from one of my communication classes. I live in Charleston, South Carolina, and we get a lot of hurricanes. That means a lot of rain. After Hurricane Matthew flooded parts of the city in 2016, one of my students brought in a picture of a shark swimming around in someone's front yard. He was showing it to other students before class, telling us all to watch out for sharks if we were walking through flooded streets. As the old-man media professor and multiple-hurricane survivor in the room, I had the sad duty of telling my student that his shark picture was an obvious fake; I'd seen it passed around the internet for *years.* The real reason not to splash around in urban floodwater, I explained, is that it comes up from the sewer. And sewer water is treacherous enough without sharks sloshing through it. My student glared at me and then at his phone and then sat down. "But my friend *sent* this to me," he insisted. And maybe his friend was just trying to be helpful. That still does not a yard shark make.

WHITNEY: Here's another example a student shared in one of my media literacy classes. This student had a close girlfriend group, and they were constantly posting photos to Instagram of parties and other college whatnot. One friend only posted photos where she looked good, even if the other friends in the pictures were sneezing or seemed constipated, which the rest of the group noticed and giggled about among themselves but never mentioned to their friend.

One day, the friend posted a group photo to Instagram that she'd photoshopped to make herself look thinner. The whole image—and her friends' bodies—had been distorted as a result, making her edit and her motives, let's say, obvious. My student had been in that picture and admitted to downloading it and sending it to her other girlfriends over group chat. They thought it was hilarious. So hilarious, in fact, that someone in the chat also downloaded the image and posted it to another chat, which made that group laugh too, until eventually the image circulated back to the friend who'd posted it. She was horrified to find out that everyone had been laughing at her behind her back, and her friends were horrified to realize how upset she was. Even though they didn't mean any harm, the entire friend group had to deal with the fallout.

RYAN: Both stories are examples of information pollution, which can take the form of **polluted** information and **polluting** information. In the yard-shark story, the information is polluted. This is the more obvious type of information pollution, and you may have heard it described as misinformation (false or misleading information spread by accident) or disinformation (false or misleading information spread on purpose). When talking about mis- and disinformation, a person's motives for sharing matter; you need to know why someone shared something to accurately describe it. Polluted information, on the other hand, *doesn't* need you to know whether something was spread on purpose or by accident. It all ends up in the same goose.

WHITNEY: My student's thinstagram story includes some polluted information; the photoshopped image misrepresented their friend's body. But the friends' *sharing* of the image, which they did for fun and definitely not to lie to anybody, is an example of polluting information. This is a more subtle category of slop, as it describes information that might be cross-your-heart true or totally well-intentioned but can still have a toxic effect on big stuff like news stories, smaller stuff like group chats, and personal stuff like your emotional well-being. Even an image that isn't photoshopped, but instead just captures people in unflattering poses, could be polluting if it makes the photo's subjects feel terrible about themselves.

RYAN: The pollution concept is helpful in these cases because it directs attention to how information impacts the landscape, regardless of what the information was meant to do and what someone meant for it to mean. As we'll see throughout the book, those intentions matter much less than what ends up happening as a result.

WHITNEY: Thinking about the effects of information pollution also helps focus attention on the people who are most often harmed by it. This lines up with an idea known as **environmental justice**. For decades, researchers have shown how Black people, Indigenous people, and people of color are more likely than white people to have their air, water, and surrounding environment polluted. Just by living their lives, they're at greater risk of being poisoned.

The same basic thing is true online. People who belong to marginalized groups—which means that they face unique forms of disrespect, discrimination, and danger—are flooded with pollution in ways that others are not. Whether it's because of their race or religion or gender identity, these groups have to deal with false claims about their lives, harmful stereotypes stated as unquestionable fact, and constant violent attacks simply because of who they are. In a 2020 Pew Research Center survey, for example, many more Black and Latinx people than white people said they were harassed online because of their race, many more women than men said they were harassed because of their gender, and many more lesbian, gay, and bisexual people than straight people said they were harassed because of their sexual orientation.

This research lines up with other studies of online abuse, including a 2018 Amnesty International analysis of Twitter showing that Black women were 84 percent more likely than white women to be targeted by abusive tweets. A 2016 Data & Society report also found that racial and sexual minorities were more likely to self-censor out of fear that they would be harassed. Trans people face especially vicious harassment online; in a 2019 study, anti-bullying organization Ditch the Label and analytics company Brandwatch analyzed ten million social media posts about trans issues and found that 15 percent of all trans-related comments from 2016 through 2019 were violent and dehumanizing. If you're a cisgender reader, imagine if 15 percent of all the posts and comments made about you online were that hateful.

Using the term *pollution*, whether the information is polluted or polluting, reminds us that information isn't some abstract thing "just" on the internet. Online information can do real damage to people's bodies and offline lives—damage that some people have to deal with much more often than others.

RYAN: Although certain groups face increased pollution risks, having to navigate tons of sewer water online can be difficult for everyone. We've both been teaching classes about the internet for over a decade, and without a doubt, all the bad, weird, and hurtful information hurricaning around seriously stresses our students out. There's lots of fun stuff online too, of course, but when pollution spreads, students describe feeling anxious and worried and torn between fear of missing out and fear of being present. We see this in class discussions and also in our students' stories about their everyday online lives, often with a lot more consequence than believing in yard sharks. Our students aren't the only ones who worry, either. So many of the conversations we've had with friends and family and journalists center on how bad social media can make us feel.

WHITNEY: All this pollution isn't just stressful for individuals. It's also terrible for democracy, for one pretty important reason: democracy requires citizens to accept the same basic set of facts. Thanks to pollution, pollution everywhere, that's not always possible. Especially when it comes to things like a global pandemic, we all *need* to have the same basic set of facts. Having some people totally steeped in polluted information, but totally convinced that the sludge they're covered in is actually crystal-clear air and water, can be a real problem. It's also a real problem for all the other major offline issues we're facing around the globe, from the climate crisis to various refugee crises to the rise of nationalism and authoritarianism. When the information landscape is a mess, good luck trying to solve all the other messes, since solutions require citizens to have access to—and trust in—good information.

RYAN: In other words, information pollution is a big, collective problem. But it isn't just collective in the sense that it splashes all over the place, as a social justice issue and a political issue and an everyday well-being issue. It's also collective in the sense that we all *contribute* to it; we all do our fair share of splashing.

It's easier to understand how this works offline, so we'll start there. In our neighborhoods and in nature, the worst polluters are the ones who deliberately pollute, who do things like dump big barrels of toxic slime into a lake.

WHITNEY: Or who fling a million coffee cups into a pile in the middle of a forest.

RYAN: That would be bad and also nonsense. But the worst polluters aren't the only people generating pollution. Even people who don't try to pollute can cast off all kinds of muck and grime. For example, Whitney and I don't wake up in the morning looking for ways to destroy the environment. But we still pollute simply by going about our business.

WHITNEY: Just say "using the toilet," Ryan.

RYAN: That's only one example of what I mean! We also impact the environment when we wash our hair, drive our cars, or use plastic baggies to clean up after our dogs. People typically don't consider those kinds of things polluting because they don't *mean* to pollute. Still, the pollution flows, with all kinds of environmental consequences we can't see.

This is also true online. The most obvious problems and biggest polluters are the people who spew lies to their millions of followers, organize social media harassment campaigns, and post conspiracy theory after conspiracy theory. Those are huge sources of pollution, but they're not the only places it can flow from. Pollution also has fun, seemingly harmless sources, like group chats with your friends.

I can speak from experience here, since my oldest daughter, Sophia, is a teenager and she and her friends spend a *lot* of time in their group chats sharing jokes and gossip and memes that would make a yard shark blush. Like millions of other people in millions of other group chats, they're just talking and being silly, but pretty nasty toxins can flow through these kinds of everyday channels too. The fact that there are so many group chats, and so many people sharing so much stuff, means that when pollution enters our networks, it can really add up.

On the other hand, when we're more aware of hidden pollution and how we can absolutely pollute even when we don't mean to, we're in a better position to stop, reflect, and adjust what we were going to say. Maybe we can avoid hurting a friend's feelings. Maybe we can avoid making things worse for someone being bullied. Maybe the consequences are less clear than that, like if we simply avoid tossing this little bit or that little bit of pollution into the Redwood Adventure Park of our online networks. These things might feel small, but they can make a big difference in someone's day and maybe their life.

WHITNEY: We can only do so much individually, though. The entire business model of industrial-grade polluters is to pump out bad information, creating the perfect environmental conditions for out-of-control toxicity. You cutting back on your yard-shark sharing isn't going to fix that.

RYAN: That's a tightrope we'll walk throughout this book. We have to acknowledge and deal with the cultural, economic, and political forces that cause so many of our problems. At the same time, we can't limit our focus to what's totally out of our control. There *are* things we have some control over. There *are* some things we can do. Remembering what those things are can help us avoid accidentally feeding into supersized pollution. And when the pollution is yard-shark-sized, remembering how easily pollution spreads, and how easily we can spread it, is good practice for when the pollution is more expansive and toxic.

WHITNEY: That's the kind of practice this book will give you. We'll show you how to identify pollution risks, minimize the bad stuff you're putting into the online environment, and maximize the good stuff you're putting into the online environment. By the end of the book, you'll have lots of tools to help you do your part to keep your spaces healthier for yourself and for others.

RYAN: We got to this kind of thinking after years and years of focusing on the internet + politics + media stuff, always under a big question mark about what to do when online interactions are creative and fun and, at the same time, destructive and harmful.

The thing we've learned is that we're all, very literally, in this together. What we each do affects other people in good and bad, big and small ways. So we have to keep ideas of connection, consequence, and shared responsibility at the front of our minds. Throughout the book, we'll be drawing from our research, teaching, and everyday lives to illustrate how to do this when trying to make sense of the often confusing, always hyperconnected online world.

WHITNEY: That *hyper* part is key here, since we're not talking about connection in abstract or daydreamy ways (although personally I like talking in abstract and daydreamy ways). Our connections online are always moving, always evolving, and always threatening to transform the smallest things into enormous things.

RYAN: For us, the key to navigating all these twists and turns is **ecological thinking**. By *ecological,* we're not talking about the actual land and trees and sky. Instead, it's an orientation to the world—online and off—that foregrounds the dense interconnections between yourself, other people, and the living and nonliving things that exist within the spaces we share. Environmental scholar Timothy Morton says something similar as he traces the connections that make up the natural world—connections, he says, that are tangled up with our human world too.

WHITNEY: By reflecting on everything we're connected with on social media, we can figure out where we're standing within our networks. From there, we can zoom out, way out, from the technologies we're using, friends we're talking to, and audiences we're aware of to anticipate downstream consequences: the unexpected effects of our sharing, which we can only appreciate when we have a wider perspective. Zooming out also helps us understand how and why polluted information filters through the ecosystem to get to us, and where it might continue flowing if we choose to spread it.

RYAN: Astronauts have described a similar perspective shift, though on a much grander scale. After they see Earth from outer space, many have spoken about a newfound sense of care, concern, and responsibility for the planet as a whole. This shift in perspective is called the overview effect. The book you're holding in your hands can't rocket you to outer space, and we're sorry for that, but it can help you imagine the world in new, zoomed-out ways.

WHITNEY: What we realize when we take a broader perspective is that "all flourishing is mutual." This is a quote from environmental biologist Robin Wall Kimmerer. To illustrate this idea, she talks about the relationship between beans, corn, and squash. When all three are planted together, each contributes to what Kimmerer calls an "organic symmetry" that allows each individual plant to thrive. The corn provides a structure that the beans can climb for more sun. The beans return the favor by adding much-needed nitrogen to the soil, fertilizing the corn and squash. The squash grows at the base of the corn and beans, keeping the soil shaded and moist. All three plants thrive when all three plants thrive; when one of them doesn't, neither do the others.

RYAN: You've probably seen examples of mutual flourishing in your own life. When you're working on a group project and everyone is helping, your grades tend to be higher. Or when everyone's being chill in the group chat, your mood tends to improve. The opposite is also true. When there's bullying at your school, it's usually not just the person being bullied who ends up hurt. On social media, harmful stuff quickly becomes everyone's problem.

WHITNEY: We'll explore the consequences of connection, both good and bad, throughout the book. But before we jump into some exciting time travel to set the stage (we're not done with you yet, Redwood Adventure Park), let's take a quick moment to get a feel for what we hope this book inspires. Begin by imagining your favorite outdoor place. Maybe it's a national park you've visited with your family. Maybe it's a park down the street from your house. Maybe it's somewhere you've never actually been but have read about or seen on TV. For me, it's the Community Forest in Arcata, California, home of my undergraduate alma mater, Cal Poly Humboldt, where the redwoods meet the Pacific Ocean. I never feel happier than when I'm walking those trails.

RYAN: And for me, it's Folly Beach County Park, in South Carolina, right on the Atlantic. When you get to the park, you see wide-open ocean rolling on one side and serene saltwater marshland swaying on the other. The sight of both at once, especially as the sun sets above the marsh, stops me in my tracks every time.

WHITNEY: Whatever place you choose, imagine it on a perfect summer day. The air is sweet, everything is alive, and you're warm and safe and happy. There are people all around you who are happy too, having a picnic or running around or simply walking by without worries. That's the feeling we want to encourage—

that you're grounded somewhere you care about, surrounded by people you want to do right by. The internet can be an enormously stressful, sometimes very strange place. But it helps to remember the world we want to live in, and to do what we can to make it like that for others and for ourselves—because as you're about to learn, *others* and *ourselves* are always connected.

Redwood Adventure Park 2.0

Ecological thinking helps us understand the connections among our technologies, our networks, and one another. To show how, in this book we'll follow the day-to-day experiences of a recurring cast of characters who, like many of you, have to deal with the stressors, controversies, and of course jokes gone wrong at and around their middle school. Whitney's Redwood Adventure Park story will be our jumping-off point—but not the cup-throwing story from 2003. This version of the story takes Whitney's family road trip and time-machines it into today's social media era. Whitney is still in college; her sister Hilary is still sixteen; and her brother, David—whose middle school is central to all the book's stories—is still thirteen. Her mom, of course, is still an unrepentant cup-thrower. We'll let fictional college-age Whitney take it from here:

So, OK, there we were at Redwood Adventure Park aka Redwoods on Mars, when randomly my mom throws my sister's hot-chocolate cup on the ground. We were like what!? It was the weirdest day. And not just because of "the Awesomeness," nope, it started before that even, when one of the people who worked there told us about the mom and baby Bigfoot he saw that week (sure) and that they stunk up the forest with their urine perfume (gross). David believed him and had been trying to film a Peefoot in the woods behind us right as my mom threw the cup. So he got the whole thing on video. He edited it down and posted it to his friends' group chat, and they all thought it was pretty funny.

Clint (I love that kid) was at the grocery store with his dad when he saw it, and they re-created the cup-throwing with a cup from I don't know where, the deli maybe, which Clint then posted to the group chat too. And then Kyle (I hmm-face emoji that kid) set Clint's clip to music and posted it to TikTok.

And that's when the trouble started. Because just before David posted the cup-throwing clip, his friend Stacy (I call her Stessy because YOU WOULD KNOW WHY if you met her) had posted something to the group chat about how her dog needed to be put to sleep, which is legit sad. But David didn't know that because he was busy trying to film a Pee-foot and doesn't really pay attention to things anyway. So he hadn't scrolled up, blah blah. Still, it was LOL LOL WHAT when David apparently responded to this super sad news with a video of my mom throwing a cup. Like was he saying the dog was like a piece of trash? Was he saying it wasn't worth being sad about? Either way, it made people laugh because it was so random and also terrible.

Stessy lives on the dramatic side of life, but in this case I get it. Not only did she think David was laughing about her dog (which would have been THE WORST if he was), but suddenly everyone in the chat was talking about my mom defiling the redwoods with that cup instead of Stessy's news. So Stessy starts a new chat without David, calling him a troll, and a bunch of people end up responding, some defending David and some being like, yeah, he's definitely a troll because they didn't want Stessy to yell at them too.

And David's totally oblivious to this. Like at that exact moment we're laughing and laughing about the Awesomeness (which is literally just trees). Clint felt bad because he also responded with a cup thing, and he KNEW about the dog, so he screencapped some of the stuff Stessy was saying. But he didn't explain about the dog. He just sent the meanest comments, which David got right as we were heading back to the car. So then we had to deal with all that suddenly, yay.

1

Feeling Better So We Can Share Better

· · ·

When people talk about the environment, they generally mean what's outside and separate from the people who live, work, or play within it. But the line between inside and outside is actually a lot blurrier than we might think. The stuff that happens inside, like a furnace generating a lot of ashy smoke, impacts what happens outside, like air quality. The stuff that happens outside, like a big storm, impacts what happens inside, like power outages. Social media aren't any different, which is the topic of this chapter: how our overall well-being (what's *in here*, which Whitney identifies by pointing dramatically from her head to her toes) influences what we're sharing on social media (what's *out there*, which Ryan identifies by pointing dramatically up, down, and all around his screens). It might seem strange at first, but to make sure we're sharing in the best and most careful ways possible, we need to take care of ourselves and of others—and to understand how stress can complicate things for everyone.

Pollution Chain Reactions

Research on stress and social media helps explain the link between feeling and sharing. This work shows that our screens can be draining, like a reverse battery recharge for our minds. We feel bad when our batteries are drained, and that's bad enough. Even worse, though, evidence suggests that when we're overwhelmed and exhausted on social media, we're more likely to spread information pollution. For example, computer scientist Najmul Islam and his team found that people experiencing social media fatigue tended to share more false stories about the COVID-19 pandemic.

We've observed the same pattern in our students, particularly related to doomscrolling. Journalist Karen Ho uses this term to describe how people scroll and scroll and scroll through bad news, fear, and outrage in their feeds, despite how terrible all that scrolling through all that negativity makes them feel. As students in both our classes have explained, doomscrolling and knee-jerk sharing often go hand in hand. The more students glue themselves to their devices, they report, the more they tend to get swept up in angry, fearful, or conspiratorial reactions. And the more they do that, the more they experience anxiety and depression, trouble sleeping, and a dip in their overall well-being. So why do they keep doing it? Because, they tell us, at least those panicked reposts and retweets make them feel like they're doing *something*.

WHITNEY: Here's a front-row-seat classroom example. The semester the COVID-19 pandemic hit, I was teaching a media literacy course. As rumors about the virus and potential campus shutdown spread, our discussions centered on what students were encountering on social media and how they were responding. One student admitted to doomscrolling as a day job and lamented how little information she was getting from official sources. "If you're not going to give me information," she said, "I'm going to take what I have and run with it. Even if something is just a possibility, I'm still going to share it. I want people to know." This student was channeling her frustrations and fears into action—even though she knew, deep down, that the information might not be accurate. In her mind, that was still better than saying nothing. We've heard similar things from our families and our colleagues and—gasp—have even observed this impulse in ourselves.

RYAN: We sure have. During fall 2020, I was at max stress. COVID-19 was raging and so was the presidential election, and I was mostly stuck in my home without much to do but teach my Zoom classes and worry. So a lot of afternoons, I'd melt into the couch to check in with Twitter, panic over what I was seeing, then text my brother the most upsetting posts. More than a few times I needed to text him a correction not long after hitting send because I had missed some details or context—like when I sent him pictures of the post office supposedly removing public mailboxes to make it harder for people to vote by mail. In reality, the mailboxes were being switched out for routine maintenance. But just like Whitney's student said, sharing the bad news (or what I thought was the bad news) made me feel less helpless, at least for a moment. After that moment, I could see that I hadn't been helping anyone.

Social media stress is, of course, specific to social media. But anyone who has been really tired or hungry or overwhelmed has probably had similar kinds of offline experiences. This is standard brain stuff, as neuroscientist Amishi Jha explains. When we feel frazzled and our heads are full of stormy thoughts, our attention—exactly what we need for evaluating information and making careful choices—is significantly weakened. We also lose the ability to regulate our emotions. We simply don't have the cognitive fuel. So when stress goes up, we're much more likely to do something we end up regretting, like snapping at our parents or friends or yelling at the animals we live with because UGH EVERYTHING.

Whether they happen online or offline, stress reactions are powered by our limbic brain, also described as the lizard brain. In terms of human evolution, the lizard brain is the oldest part of our brain and is responsible for assessing threats and keeping us safe. When the lizard brain perceives danger, it starts yelling: *THREAT THREAT THREAT! This is wrong! We gotta do something!* And suddenly we're fighting, fleeing, or freezing (or posting).

Sometimes our lizard brain is right: we really are in danger and need to react immediately, like by jumping out of the way of an oncoming car. But the lizard brain, whose entire job is to scan for threats, has the tendency to be a wee bit overactive and often sees threats when there aren't any.

No matter how right or wrong it is, our lizard brain is doing its best and is trying to help us—it's our greatest, most loyal protector. But as focused as it is on being our personal guardian, it can also limit us to a super zoomed-in view. All we're aware of is THREAT THREAT THREAT. As Whitney's student explained, and as Ryan admitted, fight-flight-freeze reactions might feel right in the moment but tend not to solve underlying problems. They can even make things worse—because fighting-fleeing-freezing isn't a plan; our lizard brain isn't thinking about the future. It's only thinking about the immediate threat, or what it believes is a threat, and how it can punch its way out. Or hide.

Online, the lizard brain easily sets us up for a **pollution chain reaction**, which goes a little something like this: We're overwhelmed and post or say something from a fight-flight-freeze place. This ends up polluting other chats or feeds, either because the information is false or misleading or because the information is simply stressful—there's too much of it, or it doesn't line up with the signals others are sending us. However it's generated, our pollution contributes to others' tired frazzle, which increases the likelihood that their own guard lizard will start sharing, raising the group's pollution levels even more, raising people's stress even more, looping back to the start of the cycle. Eek.

REFLECTION Think of a time that you've been part of a pollution chain reaction. How did it get started? Did you fight, flee, or freeze? What did the people around you do?

To illustrate, here's a Redwood Adventure Park spinoff story about Neev, one of David and Stacy's classmates. He's doing his best to respond to several friends at once, but it's hard to keep track of everything. There's controversy over the cup-throwing video, a fight over a prank related to their teacher's beloved goat, Tabitha, and blowback from racist graffiti at their school (we'll explain how it all connects). Needless to say, Neev is feeling pretty lizard-brained.

Neev makes a face at his phone. What is Stacy even talking about? Something about her dog? That's terrible, but what about David? And a cup? The all-caps energy of her fifteen texts is strong. But about what? Neev does his best to keep up.

Stacy: and i was like stop trolling david

Neev: Who was trolling David

Stacy: no dabvid was trolling
Stacy: DAVID IS ALWAYS TROLLING

Neev: With a cup?

Stacy: THAT WAS HIM TROLLING
Stacy: OMG

Neev: ?

Stacy: this isnt funny

Neev is definitely not laughing. Then Jake messages about the school's latest controversy: somebody wrote racist messages on their friend Sara's locker. In response, Jake and Sara organized student protests every day this week, and Principal Smith was NOT happy. Jake asks if Neev has seen the principal's latest Facebook post about it. Neev says no, so Jake explains that it was all about needing to come together as one happy family and how the school would respond to *all* disturbances to campus, dramatic music. Like as a vague threat, like students saying the school needs to do something about the racist graffiti is as bad as the racist graffiti?

Neev responds with a keyboard smash and sits down at his laptop to look for the principal's Facebook post. And sure enough, there's Old Baldy waggling his fingers at the students protesting the racist graffiti, which he didn't wag so much when the graffiti was there, but OK.

Stacy keeps messaging, though now it's shifted to iMessage. She's . . . everywhere.

Stacy: i'm sooooo mad

Neev: im sorry

Stacy: and clint was like he didn't mean anything it was just a cup joke
Stacy: THATS CALLED TROLLING CLINT

Neev: wait he was trolling clint

Stacy: NEEV

Before Neev has a chance to respond, not that he wants to, the algebra group chat pings. There had been commotion earlier between third block and fourth block after Mrs. Bishop told another story about her goat, Tabitha, in class. She was constantly talking about that goat, and every time she did, students would go into meme-making *hyperdrive. This time, though, it wasn't just memes. Norah started impersonating the goat in the main chat, and Orin and Kyle plus a few others in third block thought it would be funny for people to pretend like they believed it was actually Tabitha. Clint had texted Neev with a screencap of the plan, which Neev thought was the most Orin-sounding scheme he'd ever heard.*

Norah adds another goat joke to the algebra group chat just as Stacy jumps back into their chat. Neev's iMessage looks like a pinball game.

> Stacy: do u think it's ok to throw a cup a dog
> Stacy: ???????

Neev clicks back to the fourth-block group chat. For people who constantly complained about Mrs. Bishop's goat stories, they sure never stopped talking about goats. Then another message from Jake. The principal is dragging Jake and Sara to his office?

Neev wants to show his support but isn't sure what to say; it's all so serious. So he doesn't respond. Meanwhile, the algebra group chat keeps pinging, goats and goats and goats. Norah says that Neev was in the other chat too (which one? Neev can't keep it straight) and was laughing (he was?) and what did he think. What did he think? Another message from Stacy comes in, but Neev doesn't read it. Too many words.

"I think people in third block are a-holes," he types. His face gets hot. Why did he say that? He quickly adds a "jk," then closes his laptop.

Neev is juggling multiple threads with multiple issues. Together, they're enough to push him into overwhelm. As his lizard brain kicks into high gear, Neev freezes with Stacy, flees from Jake's troubles, and fights with the algebra-class group chat. In every case, his reactions risk adding to everyone else's piles of sludge.

In this case and so many others, the problem isn't the information itself. The problem is the lizard brain's fight-flight-freeze reactivity, which zooms us in on the thing right in front of us. In the process, we tend to lose track of what caused what, how important certain problems are, and what the most helpful response might be. When that happens, our actions—however good our intentions are and however justified we might feel—are more likely to backfire. It's a pollution chain reaction just waiting to happen.

Taking Care, Gaining Perspective

There's one solution to the kind of reactivity Neev is experiencing, and that's perspective. Perspective allows us to identify causes, evaluate how big a deal something really is, and make thoughtful choices that consider other people's feelings and circumstances. This is much easier said than done, of course. Once the lizard brain grabs us by the feet, it's very hard to kick ourselves free. The question is, when that happens, what can we do to zoom back out?

The first step is to pay close attention to our body, which sends all kinds of helpful signals that we're becoming reactive. This is our sympathetic nervous system at work, which sounds like it should be nice but, according to *Harvard Health*, is the "gas pedal" for the lizard brain's fight-flight-freeze response. The sudden surge in stress hormones results in an increased heart rate and rapid breathing; other symptoms can include a tight chest, a lump in our throat, a hot face, and sweating.

Often, we shift into lizard mode before we realize it's happening. This is a pretty neat feature of our nervous system, since true threats, like the oncoming car we mentioned, tend to come out of nowhere. In these cases, our physical reactions need to be faster than our mental awareness. But the speed at which this happens can also make it difficult to notice that we've become reactive when we're not faced with a life-or-death threat. It can take someone accusing us of being snappy to know we're feeling snappy, and even then, we might get irritated that they're suggesting we're irritated!

This is why it's important to focus on what our body is doing. If suddenly our heart rate goes up, our face gets hot, and we start to sweat, that's our cue to go check the front door, because it's very likely that our lizard brain will be waiting for us, velociraptor grin wide, holding a pie.

Once we realize our sympathetic nervous system is in overdrive, we can keep stress responses in check by activating its calmer twin, the parasympathetic nervous system. If the sympathetic nervous system is a gas pedal, the parasympathetic nervous system is a set of brakes—it slows down the fight-flight-freeze response. Long deep breaths from your belly are a simple but effective way to pump the brakes, and there are lots of other strategies too; you can experiment to see what works best. Other possibilities include repeating a calming phrase, praying, or doing a quick body scan (where you pay attention to different points on your body starting with your feet to the top of your head)—whatever feels most soothing. And it doesn't need to take a hundred hours, either—a few minutes of taking care can do a whole lot to slow you down, which can stop or reduce zoomed-in lizard-brain reactivity.

Once you feel you've gained a bit of perspective, or at least once your heart isn't beating so fast, you can ask yourself a few wellness check-in questions:

1. **What is my body saying "no, thank you" to?**
   This question is taken from the infinite wisdom of Whitney's three-year-old nephew, who, when he was asked why he doesn't like oatmeal, answered, "Because my body says 'no, thank you.'" It might seem funny at first, but Whitney's nephew was onto something. Asking this question allows you to reflect, without self-judgment, on what's making you feel uncomfortable.

2. **What do I need in this moment?**
   Some alone time? Someone to talk to? A particular activity?

3. **Who can help me, and what could they do?**
   Maybe your friend could kindly stop sending you so many messages. Maybe your parent could come sit with you. Maybe your dog could come outside with you and chew on twigs while you look up at the clouds.

WHITNEY: I've navigated serious anxiety all my life (it's just how my brain is), so I've needed to develop strategies for responding mindfully when my stress response goes into overdrive. For me, moving my body really helps, so when I hear my lizard brain knock, I stop, drop, and roll over to my yoga mat. Or I go for a walk and focus on what I can hear, which is a way to disrupt the mean, upsetting, and often downright scary stories—about something going wrong, about getting sick, about someone I care about randomly deciding they hate me—that my lizard brain has the very rude tendency to tell me over and over again even though they make me hyperventilate.

I used to get mad about this, but now I realize that old Lizzie is just trying to warn me about something that it thinks needs my attention. In between listening to the birds and wind, I tell it, "Thank you for caring, but I'm actually OK right now," which is something I learned from the psychologist and meditation teacher Tara Brach. That has helped enormously and means I'm not constantly in a fight with myself.

RYAN: I don't experience anxiety in the same way Whitney does; instead I get overstimulated easily, which can send me into a lizard state before I even know what's happening. When there are lots of items on my to-do list, lots of pings to my messaging apps, or lots of noise when I'm home with my kids, my natural instinct is to handle it all at once. Having unfinished tasks makes my bones hurt. But when I push too hard to do it all, I lock up and shut down and then I can't do any of it (my chest gets tight from just reading Neev's story!).

So I've developed strategies for focusing on what I can handle in the moment and letting the rest wait. I switch my phone to Do Not Disturb. I set schedules for when I'll only work on certain things. I put on big headphones, play some comforting music, and go into a quiet room for a few minutes. And I've learned to vocalize that I'm feeling overwhelmed instead of just letting it freeze me up. My kids now know the answer to "How many things can Dad do at once?" ("Jussssssttt onnnne"). And Whitney now knows what it means when we're at a loud academic conference and I say, "I have to take a walk and buy a chai latte."

In a perfect world, you'd be able to explain what you need when you need it to the people around you, and they would be happy to help. But that's not always possible. It may be that *they* are reactive, lack perspective, and can't help in that moment. Still, noticing your physical responses to stress, recognizing when you need to put on the brakes, and giving yourself the care you deserve is a powerful practice. It makes you feel better, for one thing. For another, it can help prevent you from causing or intensifying a pollution chain reaction in others.

REFLECTION List some activities that relax you and make you feel content. Cross out the ones that require travel or lots of time and equipment, and focus on things you can do right away. Rewrite the list and put it somewhere you'll remember. Then when you start feeling stressed out, you'll have some good options for putting on the brakes.

Oxygen Masks and Lizard Brains

Noticing physical stress responses, recognizing limits, and offering care is something you can do for others as well. The benefits to them are the same as the benefits to you: it's better to feel better, and also, feeling better can help minimize the pollution we spread. We would not, however, advise that you try to care for others when you're feeling lizardy yourself.

Why? For the same reason that airline passengers are told to put on their own oxygen mask first if the plane loses cabin pressure. This isn't because of me-first selfishness; it's because you can't effectively help others put on their masks if you're gasping for air. This is equally true of lizard-brain reactivity. So make sure your mask is on securely before trying to respond.

The first and most basic tip for helping others is to avoid jumping to conclusions when someone says something that seems like an insult or accusation. It would have saved everyone a lot of trouble if Stacy had followed this suggestion. To apply this tip when you feel attacked, repeat back what you think the person is saying before you add any commentary. This will give them a chance to clarify their meaning. You might find that they meant something very different from what you assumed. If you still feel hurt, rather than pointing a finger at what you assume they meant to do, explain how their words or actions make you feel. This will give them another chance to explain where they're coming from. The goal is for both people to speak honestly and respond to what's actually happening, rather than reacting to what they *think* is happening.

To help support a reactive person, a second tip is to ask the other person the three wellness check-in questions listed above. What is their body saying "no, thank you" to? What do they need? Is there anything you can do? Then—and this is the most important thing—respect their wishes, especially if what they ask for is space and quiet. Both Neev and Stacy could have used this tip to avoid spinning out into an argument.

When pollution is already flowing, these tips will help minimize and maybe even reverse the damage. But preventing pollution from spreading in the first place is better than even the best cleanup strategies. Maintaining boundaries with the people in your life is one way to do this. The term *boundary* might sound negative or even antagonistic, like the line two quarreling siblings draw down the middle of their bedroom to make sure the other sibling doesn't touch anything that isn't theirs. That's not what we mean here. Instead, boundaries are about clearly stating what your nos are, so you can fully enjoy your yeses. The benefits of saying no go beyond your own comfort; a direct, respectful "nope, sorry, can't/won't" also prevents another person from having to do backflips trying to figure out what you need and want. This can cut down on all kinds of pollution. For example, if Neev had made his boundaries clear to Stacy, even just by saying that he needed a few minutes to himself, he could have avoided making her even angrier when he couldn't give her the energy (and sympathy) she needed. Then they could have revisited the conversation when they were both a bit calmer.

We can speak personally to the benefits of clear boundaries. We've worked on three books together, always remotely, and these days we have a great system for writing, discussing daily tasks, and negotiating schedules while also doing normal friend stuff like talking about our dogs. (Hey, Everett! Hey, Backpack!) But things didn't run so smoothly at first. When communication broke down—and that happened a lot (hi, we're pretty different)—we'd both end up stressed out. Very often, that stress would splash onto other areas of our life.

WHITNEY: For example, I'd regularly make Ryan's head fall off when I'd send five-hundred-paragraph text messages on a Saturday morning because I had a GREAT idea about our latest project and wanted to know what he thought IMMEDIATELY (this was especially a problem back when I was flying into limbic panic without the safety net of yoga or walking meditation; it was free-range lizard brain all the time).

RYAN: And I'd regularly make Whitney's head fall off when I'd not respond to her five-hundred-paragraph messages because I was running around after my kids and couldn't hold any other thoughts in my head besides making sure they didn't burn the house down (this was especially a problem back when I was shutting down from overstimulation instead of checking to see if my lizard brain was holding a pie on the front stoop).

We needed to find a way to avoid the stressing and splashing, so over time we developed a set of strategies designed to prevent frustration and the pollution that accumulates when the stuff people send each other (or don't) gets supercharged with annoyance.

First, we've found it helpful to use a *green/yellow/red* check-in code when we first start chatting live. The code works like this: You make real-time contact with a friend over text. You then ask them what color they are. If they say *green*, you can start yakking away. If they say *yellow*, let them know what you want to talk about and see if they have time or energy to discuss. If they say *red*, tell them to message you when they can, and then say goodbye (and of course, you can use any other code you agree on that indicates *available/a little bit busy/I can't talk*). Note: This code is meant for everyday situations, not emergencies. If something terrible happens, or if you're in crisis, *green/yellow/red* matters much less. For day-to-day chatting, though, this code is all about maintaining healthy boundaries. It allows another person to communicate their yeses and nos and prevents you from accidentally making someone else feel trapped. Just because *you're* willing and able to talk doesn't mean that others are too.

Stress code words are another helpful strategy we've used. Before any conflict happens, each person chooses a special code word that signals "I care about how you feel and what you think, but I'm at my limit right now and can't talk about this anymore. Give me a little space and we can revisit it later." This is helpful because when you're moving into a reactive state or are already reactive, it can be very difficult to clearly explain what you need—your lizard brain is *not* a skillful communicator regardless of whether you're talking online or in person. Its skill is in snapping, ghosting, and locking up. Having a code word allows you to explain a complex idea quickly and effectively and prevents you from doing something that will only make the situation worse.

Checking in with the other person (and with yourself) to see if there's a better way to communicate is a third strategy we've developed. For example, maybe instead of texting when you're talking about something serious, you could talk over video chat. Or maybe instead of talking over video chat, you could text. No one way is objectively better. The issue is that different apps and platforms have different benefits and drawbacks depending on the situation. The basic design of the app (like not being able to see someone's expression) might set you up for conflict. Or maybe those design elements (like having to look someone in the eye) might feel stressful to the other person, even if they're perfectly comfortable for you. Having a conversation about how you want to talk will help make the actual talking that much easier.

REFLECTION Did our communication problems remind you of any friends or family members? What kinds of conflicts have you needed to navigate because of crisscrossing pollution? How did you navigate them?

We developed these strategies to avoid stressing each other out. What we've found is that working on healthy boundaries in our own relationship has positively impacted our other relationships too. Ryan has an example.

My brother and I both have PlayStations, and we play a lot of games online together. That's one of the ways we bond and hang out. But sometimes when I'm tired, after all the kids have gone to bed, I want to play a video game by myself. Something that's one player, because I don't want to talk to anyone else; I just need to relax.

But on the PlayStation, you can message and talk to other people over voice chat, and for a while I was having this problem where it would be 10:00 p.m. my time, 9:00 p.m. my brother's time, and a message would pop up and say, "Eric Milner started a voice chat with you," with no text message or anything before, no kind of like, "Oh, hey, are you around? Do you feel like chatting?" Just like, boom, a voice chat. And I'd be in this awkward position of, Do I ignore the voice chat and make him feel bad, or do I get on and talk and make myself feel bad or make him feel bad anyway if I end up being short with him because I don't want to talk? Both options made me feel tight-chested.

So 10:00 p.m. would roll around and I'd sign in to the Play-Station as invisible in case Eric was on, just to avoid the issue. But then he wanted to know why I wasn't playing anymore; it was a whole thing. I ended up thinking, "OK, this is the kind of pollution that isn't lies or harmful information; it's the kind where you're overwhelming someone, or putting too much out there, or not adapting to the signals you're being given." So I asked him, "Could you text before you start a voice chat and I'll let you know if like, 'Oh, sorry, bro, I can't talk tonight'?" And that really helped. Now 10:00 p.m. is time I have to rest for the next day of running around, if resting is what I need.

In this case, Ryan noticed that he was slipping into an old reactivity habit: feeling like he had to immediately reply to a ping just because a ping came in, and then panicking when he didn't have the bandwidth to respond. His lizard brain might not have pushed him to fight with his brother, but it did push him to flee by signing on as invisible. He took care of himself by asking the three wellness check-in questions. First, he noticed that his body was saying "no, thank you" to feeling awkward about either ignoring his brother or being trapped into doing something he didn't have the energy for. Second, he identified that what he sometimes needed was quiet time to decompress from the day. Third, he asked his brother to check in beforehand, so he could actively choose to talk or not talk.

● ● ●

The moral of Ryan's story, and all the stories from this chapter, is that when we care for ourselves, we're better able to care for others. We're also in a better position to see the lizard brain at our doorstep, take a few deep breaths (or go pet a dog), and then decide how we want to respond—rather than being hijacked by how our lizard brain wants us to react. The same goes for our friends and family. Less lizard-brain reacting and more ecological responding makes things so much easier.

Of course, there's not a solid line dividing the networks we belong to and the networks we don't—certainly not when pollution starts a-flowing. Sludge in the form of bad information and sludge in the form of too much/weird/stressful information splashes across public and private, close friends and randos alike. This is why minimizing pollution chain reactions within our own networks is so much bigger than ourselves, our friends, or our family. Less pollution *here* can mean less reactivity *there*, and less reactivity *there* can mean more perspective *here*. More perspective, in turn, is what creates the conditions for greater calm everywhere, bringing us back to Robin Wall Kimmerer's idea that all flourishing is mutual. In our hyperconnected world, small calm moments can add up to something big. They're what make mutual flourishing possible.

2

The Four Winds of Social Media

• • •

Orin looks into the camera on his laptop. "Hey, YouTube," he begins, before regaling his twenty thousand followers with the latest edition of "Moments with Tabitha: Goat Trollings," a recurring feature of his channel in which he posts screencaps of chats and short, secretly filmed videos from class related to his various goat shenanigans. Mrs. Bishop has no idea that her goat, Tabitha, is basically an influencer now (or if she does, she hasn't said anything about it); some kid in England sent Orin a photoshop just this morning of Mrs. Bishop and Tabitha clothes shopping at a secondhand store, which had been a joke from last week's video.

Orin is particularly pleased with this week's installment, as fourth block sure was mad when he and Kyle convinced third block to act like they were fighting about believing that Tabitha actually had a TikTok. He was definitely going to get some new followers from this one. "Your behavior is disrespectful to goats everywhere," he begins, reading one of Kyle's fake comments. He pauses, then bursts out laughing.

When Orin posts goat-trolling videos for his followers, when you post your own content, or even when you like, rate, and subscribe to the content of others, a whole lot of stuff is happening besides the thing you're posting or responding to. What you experience online, what's even *possible* online, is shaped by a series of powerful network dynamics. These dynamics are like the wind blowing leaves around in the fall. You can't grab hold of the wind itself, but you know it's there because of the leaves flying all over. We call the winds that blow on social media the four *A*s: **affordances**, the **attention economy**, **algorithms**, and **assumptions**.

In addition to showing how the four winds of social media impact what you encounter online, this chapter will show how they impact what you *don't* encounter, which can be every bit as important as the stuff right in front of you. Focusing on the winds' invisible influence allows us to apply ecological thinking to all the stuff-on-top-of-stuff we find on social media. When we aren't thinking ecologically, aren't reflecting on the forces shaping the landscape, and aren't considering what information we might be missing, we're that much more likely to be blown someplace we don't want to go. So let's start pointing out the winds.

Affordances

The first *A* stands for *affordances*. The word *affordance* describes what users are able to do with a specific technology or platform. In addition to allowing users to do certain things, affordances make some behaviors more likely than others. For example, pencils (they're a technology too!) allow people to write things down. So that's what people tend to do with pencils, rather than, say, building a model train with them or wearing them as jewelry. You could technically do both things, like if Whitney wanted to make Ryan a pencil necklace for Arbor Day (which would be in very poor taste, when you think about it), but you'd need to modify the pencils in a bunch of ways to get them to do what they weren't designed to do.

The affordances of digital media allow people to caption, edit, and remix media; chop up parts of a song, video, or TV show without destroying the original file; and save, store, and access the media for later. There are also affordances related to sharing. These include reposting and retweeting, copying and pasting, and other ways people can take something they find in one spot and zip it over to another spot with a single click.

Affordances allow us to do lots of fun and creative things online; just ask Orin and the other third-block goat trolls (not to mention Orin's YouTube audience), who use all kinds of media to make all kinds of jokes about Mrs. Bishop and Tabitha. They also allow us to take things out of context; just ask Mrs. Bishop, who would likely be horrified to know that clips of her stories were circulating on YouTube and inspiring international goat memes.

For a non-internet example of context and what happens when it's lost, imagine that you're sitting in your living room with your family or close friends. Because they've known you for so long, they can instantly tell when you're in a bad mood. Maybe it's how you're looking out a specific window or how you're wearing your favorite hoodie. Your position, your demeanor, and the history you have with your loved ones fill in the blanks of what you're not saying and help them understand, first, what's going on with you and, second, what you might need. Now imagine that you're suddenly transported to somewhere unfamiliar, like a random grocery store in a town you've never been to, or the hallway of a high school you've never seen before. Those surroundings don't have a history that helps decode you, and people can't easily understand your situation or needs just by observing you.

The same thing happens when a video or GIF or meme is taken out of context; you can't know much about it through simple observation, and you can't know much about where it came from, either. This has a few tricky effects online.

The first is called **Poe's Law**. Now, Poe's Law doesn't have anything to do with ravens.

> **WHITNEY:** Ryan doesn't think that joke is funny, or that it's even a joke, but I laughed.

It's not an actual law, either. It's named after someone posting to an early 2000s web forum under the screen name Poe (hence "Poe's Law") who observed that, online, it can be very difficult to tell if something is said seriously or as a joke. Poe was right; we often have no way of knowing what someone means just from what they post, especially when we don't know them personally. Even more questions emerge when a meme or video or comment—again, especially when posted by a stranger—is taken from a place where the context had been clear and put someplace new where the context is missing.

A second related complication of affordances is **context collapse**. Context collapse happens because of how easy it is to share things and, because of that, how easy it is to take those things out of context. Lots of easy sharing combined with lots of lost context makes online audiences totally unpredictable, since you never know who's going to end up finding something once it spreads. For example, Orin might assume that only his classmates and followers know about his "Moments with Tabitha" goat-trolling series. But maybe Mrs. Bishop watches all of them. If she does, then something Orin thinks is harmless fun in one context (joking behind a teacher's back) collides with another context (insulting a teacher to her face). That might result in real troubles for Orin (not to mention real distress for Mrs. Bishop).

Orin is hardly unique in that uh-oh possibility; Poe's Law + context collapse can cause all kinds of problems for all kinds of people. Let's say you stumble on a jokey meme about a natural disaster or famous person's death and post it to social media. You know the meme is pretty mean, but you want to talk about it or laugh with your closest friends about it. If they end up sharing your post with others, or if someone else screenshots what you post and decides to share that, the entire school could end up seeing it. Maybe everyone thinks you were joking when you were being serious, or thinks you were being serious when you were joking.

When it's not clear what something is, what it means, or where it came from, it's very easy for pollution to creep in. A video or GIF or meme might look like a particular thing—a joke or something serious, a true story or a lie—but you might be wrong about that, because you don't know where it started, what it's done to other audiences, or what pollution it might have spread every time someone shared it.

When a picture or a joke or a meme is missing context, it's also easy to forget about its consequences for other people.

For example, maybe someone might not want that silly picture of them plastered across social media (or stories about their goat plastered across YouTube). Or maybe they put a lot of work into the video you and your friends are now laughing at. When we're the ones being taken out of context, we definitely notice! But when we take others out of context, we typically don't notice anything. We're just sharing a meme or laughing at a video.

REFLECTION Scroll through your phone or your social media feed. Find a meme you shared that negatively portrays someone you don't know. Do you think your feelings would change—and do you think you'd still want to share the meme—if the person featured in the image was your best friend or a family member who would be mortified that their face was being used as a punch line?

When we don't know what we're looking at or what the human impact might be, it becomes much more difficult to think ecologically. That's because we're only focusing on the things we're sharing, the people we're sharing them with, and how much fun we're having. Affordances allow us, and even encourage us, to forget about everything else. We couldn't make everything else disappear if we tried. But if we're not thinking about it, it's easy to behave in ways that can be harmful (more on that in a later chapter).

The Attention Economy

When people talk about economics, they typically mean one of two things: buying and selling things, or converting things into sources of money, a process called monetization.

You might not be aware of all the money that swirls around social media, since you don't have to pay to use social platforms like YouTube or TikTok. But money is a powerful, if invisible, influence online, and it feeds into the second *A*: the attention economy. It ensures that what you do online makes money for somebody—or a group of somebodies—when you click, like, or share things. In social media marketing-speak, this is known as engagement. You're not generating little coins every time you click on something, though. Very often, monetization is the result of the platforms selling advertisements designed for your personal eyeballs.

Here's how it works on Facebook and Instagram, two of the largest social media sites in the world, both owned by a company called Meta Platforms, Inc. When people click, post, and reply to things on either Facebook or Instagram, their actions generate data. Meta collects and analyzes this data, which it uses to sort people into categories based on their race, gender, interests, and other combinations of traits. For example, Facebook might use the data it collects to sort users into the category "women in their thirties who have kids and like soccer." The same thing happens on Instagram. Users are sorted into categories based on the data they generate, for example, "college students who like music festivals and Disney." Advertisers who want to get their ads in front of these (or any other) target customers pay Meta to make sure that their ads go to those people. Different sites can monetize users in different ways. But the process always starts with people doing things on a website and the website keeping track.

Social media content creators also make money (or at least try to) in two main ways: by working in partnership with platforms and by promoting branded content. When it comes to platform partnerships, specifics can vary; typically, ad revenue is split between the platform and the account (for instance, Orin might get a percentage of the revenue his YouTube channel generates), but there are lots of rules about who can do this and how it works. There are also rules about what content is allowed to be monetized. For example, YouTube, which is owned by the same company as Google, has a policy against monetizing hateful and violent content. But those rules aren't always enforced, and some creators have found ways around the restrictions—something we know thanks to the investigative work of data journalists Leon Yin and Aaron Sankin. Companies like YouTube might not *like* this kind of content, and they certainly talk a lot about wanting to do something about it. At the same time, monetization is a powerful force, so it's still possible to make money even from the worst videos.

Whether you're talking about social platforms monetizing engagement or influencers monetizing followers, the entire purpose of the attention economy is to get people to notice and respond to things. Orin's greeting, "Hey, YouTube!" does exactly this; it's a subtle way of saying, "You are an audience that I am trying to grow, so I will make videos I think you will want to watch, just like this one, so you'll subscribe, like, share, and comment." Just like people offline, people online are most likely to pay attention to and respond to the things that are loud and funny and scandalous. As a result, loud and funny and scandalous things do well in the attention economy. Orin isn't making videos about what a competent and normal job Mrs.

Bishop is doing; he's making videos about her goat, because it's weird and funny (at least to him, his classmates, and his followers) and therefore tailor-made for the attention economy. Of course, sometimes positive emotions succeed in the attention economy, like *squeeeee* reactions to cute animal videos. But negative emotions like outrage, disgust, or mockery go viral more easily than anything else.

While the attention economy often generates actual money, it can also generate social clout, which might not be worth dollars but is definitely worth something. Many people use social media to make themselves more visible or more liked by more people, even if they're not literally cashing in. They do this by collecting followers like Pokémon or by posting things to get a response. Or both, like when Kyle posted fake outrage about Tabitha, knowing it would get the biggest reaction. Here too, the content that tends to do the best is content that activates strong emotions, whether through audience laughter or *awwwwww* cuteness or *grrrrrr* anger.

REFLECTION Have you ever adjusted what you were going to post on social media to maximize the number of likes you got? Have you ever strategized about what to post to a group chat because you wanted to make sure people paid attention? Have you ever taken something down because it didn't get enough likes?

The attention economy is why social media are fun and interesting and keep you clicking. But there are downsides. First, because the attention economy favors the most clickable content, and because that clickable content is often extreme in some way (extremely silly, extremely annoying, or extremely polluting), it tends to hide things that are calmer, quieter, and not polluted. All kinds of people are having all kinds of thoughtful, careful discussions online. But those conversations tend not to be very visible, because they're not very clickable, because nobody is yelling or sobbing or howling with laughter in response. This can send the false message that the only things happening are hashtag extreme.

Beyond that, the attention economy can discourage ecological thinking. The reason is the basic commandment of the attention economy: "Thou shalt not NOT click." All this clicking is *valuable*. It makes social platforms money and makes content creators money too. From a business perspective, there's not much reason for platforms or content creators to say, "Actually, it would be better if you all stopped engaging with this goat-trolling video today, because it might make Mrs. Bishop feel bad or pollute people's group chats."

By nudging people to focus on the most clickable things, the attention economy—like affordances—also tends to prevent them from worrying too much about the unseen consequences of their clicks. If they suddenly did start worrying about those consequences, it could really rain on the attention economy's parade. So instead, the main decree from social platforms and content creators is that people keep clicking and clicking.

Algorithms

The simplest way to define the third *A*, algorithms, is that they're sets of instructions for completing tasks. In computing, this simple definition can get complicated fast, since some of the instructions and tasks can be extremely complex.

When people talk about social media algorithms, they're typically referring to one specific type: recommendation algorithms. As the name would suggest, recommendation algorithms recommend things. It's not always possible to know exactly what's going on in algorithms, since they're company secrets that platforms closely guard. But we see the effects of recommendation algorithms very clearly. In real time, as you watch, they show you things.

Sometimes they do this by putting specific content in front of you, like TikTok's "For You" feed that serves up preselected posts. Sometimes they provide a menu of options, like Twitter's "What's Happening" list, which gives users a set of trending stories, events, or people to read more about. In either case, your engagement is guided by the algorithm, similar to the way a docent in a museum takes you on a tour of all the different art and highlights certain things while not talking much about others.

Recommendation algorithms have ways to personalize that tour, though. They've profiled the things you've previously shown interest in—what you've clicked on, what you've liked, what you've replied to, and even what you've lingered on as you scrolled. Because they've profiled you, they can then offer you targeted, curated content. This would be like if a museum docent followed you from room to room, noted that you looked at paintings of horses longer than any other kind of painting, and then took you around to all the different horse paintings in the museum. Recommendation algorithms are designed to be helpful, especially when they guide you to something you're interested in or make it easier to find something you were looking for.

Despite this helpfulness, it's important to ask who benefits besides just you, since showing the most relevant or trendy or interesting things—whether it's a painting of a horse or a video of a teacher's goat—isn't something an algorithm does out of the goodness of its heart. Showing you relevant or trendy or interesting things is also what keeps you clicking, which is where algorithms overlap with the attention economy—since all those clicks generate dollar signs for somebody. This can be perfectly fine if what you're looking for, or what you're being recommended, is true and aligns with democratic ideals like fairness and justice for all. Or it's just a bunch of horse paintings, who cares?

Problems emerge when recommendation algorithms *aren't* just serving up pictures of horses or true, fair, and just information—when instead they recommend false, unfair, and unjust information. As an example, an investigation of a 2021 Mozilla Foundation research project on YouTube found that 71 percent of the videos their research participants flagged as harmful—from COVID-19 misinformation to conspiracy theories to graphic violence—were recommended by YouTube's algorithm. Troublingly, these videos violated YouTube's own policies against harmful content. Yet they were still being recommended. When that's where the museum docent is guiding you, the good/bad calculus shifts as fast as you can snap your fingers.

Guiding users *here* rather than *there* raises another potential problem with recommendations: the one-sidedness of the content that gets recommended. Now, when people who love horses are shown posts only about why horses are great and never about why, for instance, they stink or that their heads make them look like alligators (we're just speculating; we like horses too), one-sidedness might not seem that bad. But having only one side of a story can be very bad indeed: it can mislead people and keep them from stepping outside their own perspectives. Think about Neev and Stacy's fight. If all you're hearing is Stacy's side, or all you're hearing is Neev's side, you'll probably end up with a false, or at least an incomplete, understanding of what happened. Same thing with algorithmically recommended content. If you hear only one side of a debate, how can you make an informed decision about what to believe?

But we have to be careful when warning about one-sidedness too. Some issues have only one side! At least only one true and moral side. Racial justice is one example. Racism against Black people, Indigenous people, and people of color is real, and anything that contributes to inequality or to white supremacy needs to be called out and actively resisted. A person could say that racism in the US is a relic of the past, but it's not. Direct racist attacks still happen way too often, and systems that discriminate against and limit opportunities for people of color are a present-tense problem. Here, showing "both sides" of the issue would spread pollution by suggesting that false ideas about racism are equally as valid as the reality of racism. If an algorithm did that, it would be a problem. So, there are two sides to algorithms' one-sidedness, and that's one of the tricky things about algorithms.

As you might have already guessed, all this trickiness can discourage ecological thinking. When we think ecologically, we expand our perspective and consider how our actions might impact other people. Algorithms often do the opposite by narrowing our attention to just the stuff being recommended to us, and just the people who already agree with us. So we might think we understand the consequences of sharing, because the people whose opinions we care most about are saying the same things. Depending on who those people are, that could be OK. But what if they believe false and harmful things? What if they're bigoted? What if they don't care if Mrs. Bishop ends up feeling embarrassed or hurt, and in fact hope she does, because that would make them laugh? Our posts might seem good and normal to them, but outside that little corner, what we're sharing could do enormous damage. We could expose whole new audiences to information pollution, causing some people to begin searching for related content. This could encourage another algorithmic docent to scurry over and bring those people to increasingly ugly places. Or we could force groups of people to see something that hurts or dehumanizes them.

Anything that limits our perspective risks opening the pollution floodgates. Algorithms can—they don't always, but they *can*—do exactly that, but even worse, they can make us think we've seen everything there is to see because we've done our research. When we feel like we've put in the work, we're less likely to question if there's something else we should be worried about. That's a pool party of pollution just waiting to happen.

Assumptions

The first three *A*s describe what the winds of social media are. This *A*, assumptions, helps explain why the winds blow the way they do. This is where social media winds and actual, outside, fall-leaf-blowing winds are most different. No person created the offline winds; no person designed how they would blow. Online, the winds were created by many people and were designed to blow in certain ways, which has influenced what kinds of networks have flourished and what kinds of behaviors have been tolerated or even rewarded. This is why exploring assumptions is so important. Orin, for instance, might make his own decisions about what to post or laugh at online. But he's only able to make those choices because of all the other choices, big and small, that designers and funders and executives made about what would and should be possible on their platforms.

ASSUMPTION 1

One major assumption is the idea that *more information is always better*. This assumption was central to the creation of today's largest social platforms. Information can be a very good thing, obviously. It's how we develop new knowledge and make sure we're not believing claims without evidence. On social media, however, the belief that more information is always better than less information, and that limiting how information spreads is always *bad*, has generated massive amounts of information pollution.

As we discussed in the introduction, everyone has encountered information pollution online. But some people encounter more pollution more frequently with much worse effects, looping us back to the idea of environmental justice. The basic idea is that Black, brown, and Indigenous people, women and girls, and members of the LGBTQ community, as well as other marginalized people, are disproportionately impacted by harmful information online. For members of these communities, simply being in public can be dangerous. The result is that, online, information isn't going to feel neutral by default, because it *isn't* neutral by default. Depending on who you are, information can be harmful. Information can be a weapon.

But the experiences of marginalized people weren't the experiences social media decision makers built into their platforms. Instead, when the largest platforms were created, people in positions of power had a broadly positive relationship with information. That's not surprising. As mostly white men, they weren't likely to be *harmed* by information, definitely not by the same patterns of toxicity that marginalized groups have always had to navigate—and not just online, offline too. Because their relationship with information was a big thumbs-up, these decision makers' main worry wasn't about how to slow that information down when people were threatened. It was to figure out ways to speed information up across their platforms.

These decision makers weren't supervillains, and they didn't set out to harm marginalized groups or anyone else. They were trying to build good networks—at least, what counted as good networks based on the assumptions they were making. Assumptions, by the way, that rarely included the perspectives of people who weren't like them, who weren't included in the decision-making process. So while out-of-control information pollution—and all the environmental justice issues it can churn up—wasn't the goal when these platforms were first created, that has been the effect.

ASSUMPTION 2

The funny thing is, these decision makers probably *did* think there were protections in place, bringing us to the second assumption that's shaped social media: that the "marketplace of ideas" will correct bad information.

The marketplace of ideas is a very old concept. It describes how people go "shopping" for their beliefs by browsing all the noisy, crowded shelves in the market. Everybody who's anybody is there trying thoughts on, comparing one argument to another, before making an informed decision about what to believe. Through this process, the story goes, the best ideas end up the bestsellers and become more widely adopted throughout society; the worst ideas ultimately fade away because, well, nobody is buying them.

If all the arguments and all the evidence were available to people equally, then maybe assumptions about the marketplace would match up with how the marketplace works. As it is, only some arguments and some evidence are stocked on its shelves, and only some of those shelves are reachable by all customers.

Imagine a raucous flea-market-vibe warehouse store from your nightmares. All around, mustachioed snake-oil salespeople blast conspiracy theories into the crowd with a confetti cannon, powerful platforms fling bad ideas down the aisles like Frisbees, and try-hard influencers entice customers with free samples of empty-calorie snacks. The good ideas are there, but they're way up on the top shelves, and you have to find your own ladder.

A perfectly orderly, perfectly fair marketplace of ideas falls flat in everyday situations as well, for the simple reason that people aren't listened to or taken seriously equally across society. For some people, being heard and responded to appropriately is a given. They say something to peers or authority figures and are believed, treated respectfully, and helped without question. Other people could point to a burning building, scream "FIRE!" and be utterly ignored, either because nobody notices them standing there or because they look or think or act differently, so they aren't believed.

If you happen to be someone who other people—kids or teachers or doctors or police officers—listen to automatically, it's important to remember that there are probably people you know who are walking around right now feeling frustrated and unheard because their skin isn't the "right" color, or they don't practice the "right" religion, or they're not speaking with the "right" accent, or they aren't presenting as the "right" gender—the list goes on. If you happen to be someone who other people *don't* listen to automatically because of your skin color or religion or accent or gender presentation, you don't need to be reminded of how frustrating that can be; not being heard is what you have to deal with constantly. The marketplace of ideas forgets about this kind of unfairness and assumes that everybody's perspectives are given the same chance to be considered. The problem is, they aren't.

Online, algorithms have made this unfairness even more noticeable, since certain kinds of people (the ones who already have larger audiences) and certain kinds of messages (the ones that the attention economy favors) are most likely to be recommended and therefore seen, heard, or shared. Social media decision makers might have assumed that ultimately, with so much information everywhere, the best information would be the winner. But the information that wins most often is the information that algorithms and the attention economy boost to the top of people's feeds, while other smart stuff or thoughtful stuff or stuff that's important to you gets hardly a response. The result is a marketplace that definitely benefits some but poisons others.

ASSUMPTION 3

Assumptions about information and the marketplace of ideas connect to a third assumption that's shaped social media. And it's a doozy; it's about freedoms.

Now, most of us would agree that freedom is important. In the United States, where many influential social platforms are based, the idea of freedom is central, particularly the ideal that citizens have the right to "life, liberty, and the pursuit of happiness." This might sound simple: Who would argue with wanting to be free? But it's not that simple, because there are two ways to think about freedom. One kind of freedom focuses on individual people and emphasizes individual rights and privileges.

This is known as "freedom from" because it's about someone being *free from* outside restriction (in other words, from being told what to do). Another understanding of freedom focuses on the group and emphasizes shared needs and responsibilities. This is known as "freedom for" because it's about ensuring the same freedoms for everyone to enjoy equally.

When they were created, the largest social media platforms were most concerned with making sure that individual people were free from having their stall in the marketplace of ideas restricted. This ensured that the right to spread pollution was given a jauntier thumbs-up than the right not to be polluted in the first place.

Again, we're not talking about a bunch of mustache-twirling supervillains standing by the pollution floodgates, laughing and high-fiving as they send in wave after wave of toxic soup. Still, when speech issues have come up, especially when social platforms were created, platform decision makers have embraced and built site policies around this very particular understanding of free speech: that users should be free from having their speech policed too much.

Just like the general idea of freedom, not policing speech too much sounds OK or even good on paper. What a focus on "freedom from" often overlooks, however, is how it can actually *minimize* the freedoms for the group as a whole by creating a situation in which fewer people feel safe to speak freely.

Think about how this might work in your own classrooms. If you have one or two bullies in a class who are saying terrible things to other students, and the teacher just lets it happen because it's those students' "right" to say whatever they want, do you think you'll end up having a better class discussion or a worse class discussion? There probably won't *be* a class discussion, since many students will feel too scared to say anything. It's a strange irony: by working so hard to protect an individual's freedom to speak without consequence, you risk ensuring that there's less diverse speech, not more diverse speech, when others feel threatened or shamed or straight-up disgusted and decide they'd rather not say anything at all. This tension undermines the entire point of free speech, and in the end only benefits the polluters—with an implied "too bad, so sad" for the people they're polluting.

Together, assumptions about information, the marketplace of ideas, and freedoms helped make social media what they are today. The assumption that information wants to be free overlooked the consequences of sharing what's polluted or polluting. The assumption that the marketplace of ideas will float the best ideas to the top of people's feeds overlooked the unevenness and unfairness of how information travels across networks. The assumption that freedom means never being told what to do overlooked all the people who end up less free as a result. Our social platforms remain so messy, and very often so poisonous, because these assumptions were made but not questioned. They were taken to be a natural part of the landscape, as if all the leaves—and all the trash—were blowing around on their own.

The moral of the story is that if you're not paying attention to why the winds of social media blow as they do, you're much less likely to notice the piles of pollution accumulating around you. Until, of course, you're already up to your ankles in grossness.

On Anger

There's a final *A* to consider when reflecting on the winds of social media, and that's anger. Anger isn't itself one of the network dynamics, but it's often a consequence of them. Affordances obscure context, so it's very easy for people to jump to conclusions, be wrong, get mad, and then stir up even more anger when they lash out at inappropriate targets. The attention economy frequently rewards outrage, so it's able to circulate widely. This ropes an even bigger audience into the outrage—regardless of whether the anger is directed at the right things. Algorithms guide people to what they've already shown interest in. When an algorithm is fed riled-up clicks, angry recommendations tend to come out. Assumptions that allow harmful content to spread far and wide create puddles of infuriating slop everywhere, angering those who are forced to trudge through them. Because anger is already peeking out from behind every corner, and because the winds of social media are perfectly calibrated to make it stronger, it's no wonder that social media can feel like such an angry place.

But hold that thought, because the mere existence of anger isn't necessarily a bad thing. Anger can sometimes be positive and important. Anger can signal that something is wrong and requires action. Anger can also drive people to stick up for others and for themselves. And *not* getting angry, or being afraid of feeling anger, can sometimes cause harm. So can seemingly more positive actions like politeness, avoiding conflict, and keeping your voice down. When someone else is being threatened or harmed, inside voices, "please" and "thank you," and other bits of good manners can allow injustice to persist. A person might be trying to be nice. But how nice is it, really, when someone's refusal to push back, or their worry about making others uncomfortable, allows unfair things to keep happening?

Policing other people's anger—especially when it's in response to objectively harmful behavior like racism or sexism—can also be a problem, since the complaint "You're so angry" is often followed by "So I don't have to listen to you." Women and people of color are most likely to be shut down for being angry, especially when they're calling out injustice. In these cases, rejecting someone's anger simply because they're being loud or confrontational means that the *causes* of that anger go unaddressed—and nothing improves.

So depending on the situation, we can definitely be on Team Anger. Things get dicey when a person's anger comes from the fight-flight-freeze lizard brain, since lizard-brain responses are, by definition, zoomed in. The only thing the lizard brain is focused on is punching its way out of a perceived threat (or running away screaming from one). In reality, this perceived threat might not even be that threatening—or even slightly threatening. Our brains might be imagining things! But even when the cause of our anger is justified, the lizard brain simply isn't very helpful. When our lizard is at the wheel, the solutions we think will work in the moment rarely solve anything. Very often they make things worse—especially if we actually try to punch our way out of our problems.

This is where the winds of social media blow especially hot. To illustrate, we'll check back in with Neev, who last chapter ended up so overwhelmed by the messages bouncing across his devices that he ghosted Stacy, shut down with Jake, and called the kids in third block a-holes. Now he's got to deal with the fallout—and an angrier Stacy, who turns out to have even more going wrong than the loss of her family dog. What this story will show is how messy things can become when we're operating from a place of fight-flight-freeze *and* the winds of social media have blown us off course.

Neev doesn't really think that people in third block are a-holes; he was talking about Orin and his goat trolls, which is only like five people.

This makes Orin either mad or laugh—who can tell with that kid?—and before Neev can do any damage control, Orin takes a screenshot of the a-hole comment and posts it to the main chat. "Goat out of here," Orin writes.

And just like that, Neev's phone starts lighting up with people in third block who don't know about the goat conspiracy but do know he called them a-holes. He tries to explain: he said jk, and posts the full screenshot as proof. But that just turns into an argument about names and language even if someone is joking, which some people like Norah say is OK but other people like Aida say is rude and gets them in trouble. The more frustrated Neev gets, the more frustrated they get. And then, the old familiar tone.

Stacy: are u dead hello
Stacy: what r u doing
Stacy: i'm having the worst day

Neev: Ya you won't stop telling me

Stacy: my dad keeps yelling at me
Stacy: like i'm the one who got drunk and barfed on the jumbotron

Neev: Who barfed on the jumbotron

Neev: ?

Stacy: my sister at the football game. i told you yesterday.

Stacy: thx for listening

Neev: Ya sorry

Stacy: shes such an A hole. now my parents are so mad at me i didn't do anything

Stacy: do u eev care

Stacy: hello

Stacy: ??

Neev's chest tightens as he stares at his phone. He starts typing something mean.

Here, Stacy's anger ricochets off everyone in her path—triggered in part by a cup-throwing insult that didn't even happen how she thinks it did (same goes for the jumbotron story, but that's a tale for later). Neev's anger is a slow burn, stoked by the energy of the winds. His lizard brain rushes to his rescue, then prevents him from responding thoughtfully to his own stress or being able to care about Stacy's. Their conversation was a pollution chain reaction just waiting to happen.

• • •

Like Neev and Stacy, we all can get blown around on social media from time to time (or even more often than that). We all can end up way off course even as we're trying our best. That our networks set us up to get lost and lash out is the bad news. The good news is that we're not stuck aimlessly wandering through the complicated twists and turns of our networks. We're not helpless online, and we're not doomed to splash around in pollution for the rest of our lives. Every one of us can help make our networks healthier for ourselves and for the people we share those networks with. All we need to do is pull out our social media map and ask ourselves: Where are we?

3

Mapping the Online Environment

• • •

You've probably seen "you are here" icons before. If we were writing this book when we were your age, we'd say, "You know, like on mall directories that tell you how to get to the store that sells beanbag chairs," which was something that happened at malls in the 1990s. These days, "you are here" icons are more common on map applications, which pinpoint your location with a little blue dot or a cartoon version of your head or something; we don't know what apps you use. Whether they're in malls or on screens, the purpose of these icons is to show your current location and direct you to where you need to go next.

That's the basic idea of this chapter. We'll be using the social media map, a way of imagining online spaces, to show where you're located within your windswept networks. Three grounding ecological metaphors—redwood forests, hurricanes, and land cultivation—will guide this "you are here" mapping. As each metaphor locates you alongside the technologies, issues, and people that surround you online, they can lead you toward more informed and ecological choices about what you're adding to the figurative landscape.

You can also use the three metaphors to describe your online experiences to others. Conversely, they can use the metaphors to describe their experiences to you. Telling stories in this way can help minimize pollution chain reactions when discussing difficult issues, different beliefs about the world, and claims that aren't true. That's because first-person stories are more likely to encourage more meaningful, and less stressful, sharing than "you better listen up, because here comes the only truth that exists" assertions, which have a very strong tendency to make people feel lizard-brain reactive. Stories also encourage greater understanding of particular situations by helping people zoom out and see beyond their own perspectives—the first and most important step toward ecological thinking.

REDWOOD FORESTS

The first "you are here" metaphor is redwood forests. In the introduction, Whitney said that redwood forests are her favorite place, so this will be her story.

Just off Fourteenth Street at the edge of Cal Poly Humboldt's campus, a narrow trail leads into the Arcata Community Forest. The trail entrance, lined by tall, thin redwood trees, is bordered by a grassy field. Most mornings when I'd come to run in the forest, the trail and the field and the tops of the trees would be blanketed in a thick fog.

Entering the forest was like going back in time. I'd climb a steep hill fitted with steps made from old redwood, surrounded by trees as high up as I could see. It always felt polite to nod hello to them as they quietly, steadily, continued their centuries-old race toward the sun. One trail would lead me to another, then another, as I ran past old-growth tree stumps large enough to pitch a tent on, up and down steep gullies, and over wooden bridges.

A favorite old-growth stump on the hillside made a nice perch. When I had extra time, I'd climb the stump and sit, its cool wood slightly damp beneath me. And then I'd listen. Just a mile or so away was the ocean. I could never tell if the faint sound I heard was the wind through the trees or the waves crashing along the coast. I hoped it was the waves.

Because the redwoods are so tall, and because their branches bunch together, very little sunlight would filter down to my spot. Everywhere I'd look would be gray. But not gloomy. It can be dark in the forest, and at the same time green and vibrant. Alive. The mists and branches, trunks and ferns, mushrooms and dirt tangle together. The redwoods' woven roots do too, like veins crisscrossing the trail.

And that's just what I could see. Underground, dense webs of fungi and roots, called mycorrhizal networks, link this tree to that tree to another and another, allowing the trees to share nutrients and even communicate, at least by their standards. This makes it tricky, even strange, to separate one tree from the rest. Trees in the redwood forests aren't separate, not really, and besides that, are affected by everything else in the woods: how much it rains, how the animals are doing, and how the humans are behaving. Sitting smack in the middle of it, listening to the quiet—or was it the ocean?—all I could see, all I could feel, were those connections.

When applied to online spaces, redwood forests highlight all the stuff, from platforms to audiences, that information travels through, and all the dense interconnections that exist within those networks. This metaphor reminds us to be very careful about what we share and do, because what happens over *here*, in one social media grove, can impact what happens over *there*, in another social media grove. The four As make sure of it. Affordances help information spread far and wide. The attention economy links audiences together through the content they share. Algorithms carry that content to new places. Assumptions influence the kinds of networks that are built and how seamlessly information is able to travel.

The redwoods metaphor also helps us understand something critical about information pollution: it doesn't just *appear*. When something toxic enters the root system in nature, it's because it's been filtered in by various ecological processes. Information pollution is the same; it doesn't just show up out of nowhere. Whether the information is true or false, well-intentioned or mean-spirited, it's filtered in by the four As. Online and off, once pollution is present, it's very difficult to get rid of.

To use the redwoods metaphor to locate your "you are here" pin, you can answer the following bird's-eye-view questions, which are designed to give you the broadest possible perspective on a situation. Answering these questions will probably require a bit of research, since they ask you to describe things that you may not have personally witnessed.

- What do you know about where the information pollution came from?

- What *don't* you know about its origins?
- Which groves—audiences or platforms or communities—has the information traveled through?
- Did something within the network end up toxified or corroded?

When you reflect on these dense interconnections and how fast information can travel from one grove to the next, you're more likely to pause before you pump information into the root system.

To tell a story to others about *your* location on the map, you can answer the following first-person-view questions, which are designed to show what you personally experienced and felt in a situation. Answering these questions doesn't require any research, just honesty.

- Where did you encounter the content you're discussing?
- Who was the content shared with?
- Where did you observe it traveling?
- Did you notice any pollution as it spread?

David, for example, could tell Stacy how he came to film and post the cup-throwing video, whom he was sharing it with, and what he later found out about how it traveled through their friend group. Stacy could then respond with her own version of events, which the two could compare to better understand where the other person was coming from. Afterward, Stacy might feel better knowing that David wasn't sharing the video in response to Stacy's dog dying, and David might better understand why the video's meme-y hijack of the group chat hurt Stacy's feelings.

HURRICANES

The second "you are here" metaphor is hurricanes. In the introduction, Ryan said that the South Carolina coastline is his favorite place, so this will be his story.

I sift the sand between my toes as I look down at my phone, then out at the big rolling waves, and then back down at my phone. The blob on the radar is pretty nasty, but the pelicans soaring by don't seem to mind.

"I dunno. Everything seems fine," I think as some tourists slog behind me through the dry sand back to their beach house. "Maybe this one won't be so bad."

But later that day, the sky darkens. The air starts feeling a bit off—that kinda dense, kinda dizzy feeling that creeps in just before a storm. The high tide starts lapping up over Harborview Road. All of it is a reminder of what I've learned over the last four years as four different hurricanes approached the Carolina coast. Ocean storms are hard to predict and hard to trace because they're a highly volatile mix of wind currents and water temperature and atmospheric pressure and all this SCIENCE that churns and spins and wobbles until you've got no choice but to look at the radar, sigh, and finally admit, "All right, maybe it will be a big one."

The admission triggers a question I'm tired of asking, one I was hoping the peaceful pelicans would give me an excuse to ignore: Should my family stay, come what may, or should we pack it up and head for Aunt Lynda's house in the North Georgia hills?

I hate having to make this choice. I hate it every time.

Evacuating is stressful and expensive and disruptive, and traffic on I-26 is a gnarled nightmare. But sticking around during a volatile storm invites volatile risks. A lot can go wrong during a hurricane. If the winds miss you, the storm surge might not. If you dodge the storm surge, you still have to worry about the flooding rivers.

And that's just what Mother Nature might throw at you. Human factors make our storms that much worse. Climate change has warmed our waters, fueling larger hurricanes that stick around longer. Industrial farming has increased the pollutants that spill out into rivers when they overflow their banks. Coastal development has eroded natural marshland barriers and put booming populations right in harm's way. If my family stays home and the worst happens, we might need overworked and exhausted first responders to come save us.

Like so many times before, I feel the warning of every major risk in every little molecule all around me. We have to leave. So off we go to the North Georgia hills to weather the storm.

Online, the hurricane metaphor reflects the fact that no big controversy, story, or issue is self-contained. Like hurricanes in nature, online hurricanes are fed by many energies. This metaphor reminds us that we can't analyze a cultural storm in bits and pieces; we have to consider all the connected elements fueling it forward. The four *A*s are enormous sources of that fuel. The attention economy harnesses user engagement (made possible by affordances), which helps power a storm. As more people engage, more energy is generated; as more energy is generated, algorithms programmed to identify trending topics direct even more attention to the storm. The assumption that more information is always better feeds into the other three *A*s, adding increased energy, attention, and power.

The hurricane metaphor helps emphasize that it's not just the storm itself that spreads pollution. In nature, storm surges cluttered with debris, rivers flooded with toxins, and even water supplies contaminated with sewage allow hurricanes to spread pollution unexpectedly. Human-made structures, like high-rise condos where storm-buffering marshes once were, contribute to the damage. In the same way, online hurricanes create many chances for information pollution to be sucked in and rained down. Structures within the online environment, like algorithms, also impact how and where pollution flows when storms make landfall.

To use the hurricane metaphor to locate your "you are here" pin, you can answer the following bird's-eye-view questions:

- What underlying causes (technological, political, and economic) are feeding into a storm?
- What parts of the storm are polluted, or how might it suck in more pollution?
- Whose actions have strengthened the storm?

By asking these questions, you're able to reflect on all the elements fueling a cultural storm. When you do that, you're better able to predict what's likely to make things worse. You can also try to contain the pollution that might be sucked up or generated.

To tell a story to others about *your* location on the map, you can answer the following first-person-view questions:

- What causes did you observe, including anything you personally did or said, that contributed to the storm's creation, growth, or impact?
- Did you feel polluted by the storm, and if so, how and when did that happen?
- Did you notice that others felt polluted by the storm, and if so, was it coming from the storm itself or something else that the storm sucked up?

Say, for instance, that Mrs. Bishop found out about the feud between third block and fourth block. Getting to the bottom of things would require much more than simply blaming Orin. Lots of factors, from a YouTube audience clamoring for spicy goat content to a side conflict between Neev and Stacy, contributed to the fight. It might make for some awkward conversations, but asking each person what they experienced and locating where they saw pollution creep in would help reveal the full picture of what happened.

LAND CULTIVATION

The third and final "you are here" metaphor is land cultivation. To show the short- and long-term impact of human choices on the natural environment, we decided to highlight changes to a particular patch of land over time.

It's a warm bright day in 1930s Western Kansas. Just a few decades before, prairie grass fluttered in every direction. Now it's wheat fields, more wheat fields, and dirt. A farmhouse sits off in the distance. Something big billows on the horizon behind it. In an instant, the farmhouse is swallowed by a looming cascade of dirt a hundred feet high that plunges the perfectly sunny day into darkness. The wall of dirt roars forward, swallowing up farmhouse after farmhouse as it travels.

Dust storms such as this one plagued the Plains region in the 1930s. Not purely natural events, the storms had human-made causes too. First, new equipment allowed farmers to till the land faster—ripping up the topsoil and exposing more dirt to the elements. Second, farmers eager to turn a profit overplanted and overharvested wheat. This created a wheat surplus, which created a drop in wheat prices, which created the need to plant even more wheat to make up for the loss. And then, just as the Great Depression hit, it stopped raining. Not for one year. Not for two years. For ten. The overplowed lands dried up and fell barren. When strong winds blew, houses filled with dirt. The sky filled with dirt. All there was, was dirt.

Fast-forward to the same spot in the 1950s. There are still plenty of crop fields, though many are now lined with trees. Some are surrounded by grassland. This is the work of the US Soil Conservation Service, which, following the devastation of the Dust Bowl, restored native grasslands, planted hundreds of miles of natural windbreaks, and encouraged the adoption of more sustainable farming practices. Thanks to these efforts, the farming business is booming. So are the farm towns scattered across the prairie where farmers and their families shop and play.

But this scene doesn't last, either. By the 1990s, the land has changed again. New fertilizers, more efficient equipment, and large companies buying up small farms have transformed the prairie's patchwork of fields into miles and miles of single-row crops. Farmers—the ones left—grow literally tons of soybeans and ship them all over the world, but that messes with the local food supply and puts fewer nutrients back into the soil. It's also resulted in quieter, emptier, paint-faded farm towns. This is the push-pull—or perhaps more accurately, the push-push—between the land and the people who use it.

Applied to social media, the metaphor of land cultivation highlights how we influence our networks in big and small, positive and negative, deliberate and unintentional ways. This is true whether we're an influencer (whose land is like a large factory farm) or an everyday person with a modest follower count (whose land is like a small backyard). We can even affect our networks simply by being in them. This metaphor reminds us that everything we do online has a consequence. Here too, the four As shape the environment. Affordances are the tools people use to alter the landscape. The attention economy and algorithms ensure that when people start spreading pollution, it's able to drift into other people's networks, prompting even more people to react, in turn kicking up even more dust. Assumptions contribute to the false belief that if someone doesn't mean to do damage, they won't (but of course they still can).

Land cultivation creates all kinds of irrigation channels for pollution. Whether or not someone *means* to pollute makes little difference. Offline, people with the best intentions and the worst intentions can harm the land equally. The same is true on social media. Those who actively try to confuse, manipulate, or harm others have an obvious environmental impact; they're mass polluters. Less obvious, but no less serious, is the cumulative effect of the pollution everyday people introduce into the environment without trying. Searching for the source of this pollution doesn't mean searching for villains. It means highlighting effects and identifying causes—especially when that cause is you.

To use the land cultivation metaphor to locate your "you are here" pin, you can answer the following bird's-eye-view questions:

- How are participants in a story directly impacting their networks through active, public-facing choices like commenting on and sharing content?
- How are they indirectly impacting their networks through more passive choices that might not be public facing but which feed into the winds of social media (for example, liking, rating, or subscribing to certain social media channels, which bumps up their visibility to others and provides the content creator feedback on what their audience likes and wants to see or hear more of)?
- Regardless of what anyone intended to accomplish through their choices, what actually happened as a result?

Charting what people are contributing to the broader network makes it easier to understand what's being grown by whom and to what effects—helping identify ecologically sensitive strategies for using the land as wisely as possible.

To tell a story to others about *your* location on the map, you can answer the following first-person-view questions:

- What were your motives for doing or saying what you did?
- How did those motives influence what you shared and how you shared it?
- What happened next, as far as you can tell?

Neev and Stacy would benefit enormously from this kind of storytelling. By comparing what they both intended to do with how their actions ended up impacting the other person, they could simultaneously affirm their own experiences and honor the other person's perspective—and hurt feelings. It's hard to keep fighting once you're able to do that.

• • •

Together, these metaphors reveal three interconnected truths about social media. First, media aren't singular or self-contained. You might be looking at one GIF or image or video. But when you approach these media ecologically, you realize that everything fits within a broader context, and that those broader contexts make up the online environment as a whole.

> **RYAN:** The interconnectedness of media is why I'm such a grammar monster when my students say "social media is" instead of "social media are." The word *media* is the plural form of *medium*, yes, but more importantly, our media environment is full of countless different platforms and outlets and voices and noise. Appreciating that plurality is essential to thinking ecologically about social media.

Second, individual people are never singular or self-contained. We might have unique bodies and experiences, but we're always connected to others. They affect us, and we affect them—even when we don't realize it. Third, you can't easily separate the technologies people use from the people who use them. Technologies nudge our actions, and we nudge our technologies right back. So to understand our actions online, we need to understand the tools we use. And to understand the tools we use, we need to understand ourselves.

Understanding the connections between *this* and *that* also allows us to avoid the overly simplistic explanations (and finger-pointing) that prevent ecological thinking. However right we are, or wrong we are, or calm we are, or reactive we are, we all have "you are here" pins in the network map. Combining a bird's-eye view with lots of different first-person views exposes us to stories, insights, and dynamics that we would miss if we simply declared: "This is what I observed, and therefore, this is all I need to know." A broader view allows us to perceive the world, the people in our lives, and ourselves with greater clarity. That doesn't mean that conflict will disappear. Even if Neev and Stacy adopted all the strategies in this chapter, they would probably end up butting heads again. And there will always be people like Orin who are unwilling to give up the goat. While it's not a magical solution (which complex problems never have), "you are here" storytelling helps minimize zoomed-in thinking, which translates to better, less stressful navigation. Better, less stressful navigation means more flourishing. And more flourishing benefits everyone.

4

Sharing Information
Strategically

• • •

Sara and Jake sit in Principal Smith's office, itching to escape.

This was the third day of student protest they'd led after the school did nothing about the racist graffiti on Sara's locker, except to say some nice words about valuing diversity, which everyone knows definitely solves racism on its own (it doesn't).

Maybe they'd feel differently if the graffiti was an isolated incident. But that wasn't true. Last year, Orin and Kyle painted a bunch of swastikas on the bleachers in ketchup as a "joke" for Orin's YouTube channel and nobody did anything then either because "the rain washed it away," as Sara overheard one of her teachers say to another. It was bad, but don't worry; they were just trolling. Everybody thought Orin must have done the graffiti this time too, but Sara had heard enough stories from some of the other Black kids at school and experienced enough strange looks herself that she knew Orin wasn't the only problem.

Principal Smith's Facebook post, which he wrote after pictures of the graffiti went viral, hadn't mentioned anything about that history, though. Mostly he seemed mad that the local news ran a story about the graffiti and student protests. So Sara wasn't surprised when Smith stomped over as she and Jake were packing up their signs for the day. She was *surprised that he'd demanded to see both of them in his office. They reluctantly followed.*

Smith leans forward over his desk, his mouth set to a stern expression of I am definitely the boss. *His cheeks, however, keep flushing pink.* "Diversity is one of our core values. Diversity is one of my personal core values. That's why we have a zero-tolerance policy at this school for"— he waves toward Sara—"recent incidents. Which we're investigating." He pauses. "What we need now is to come together as a community. These protests—I understand why you're upset. I understand. But do you think unity is possible when everyone is so heated? When all anyone can talk about is what side they're on and if they're protesting?"

"I'm pretty sure we can't come together as a community when there's racists running around," Sara says. "Togetherness isn't exactly their thing."

"A bad apple." Smith nods. "We're taking the incident very seriously. There's no need to disrupt student learning more than it already has been."

"So is the problem that someone did this to Sara," Jake asks, his cheeks also flushing pink, "or that we're protesting?"

"We'll get to the bottom of it. Now it's time to lower the volume, hmm, so students can focus on their studies. That's why you're here. That's why we're all here, isn't it?"

Sara and Jake just glare.

All Aboard the Biomass Pyramid

It's not always possible to avoid spreading information pollution. In fact, vowing that thou shalt never share anything false, harmful, or stressful might do its own kind of damage. Jake and Sara's protests are an example. It might have been less upsetting—at least for the people who weren't personally affected—if everyone forgot that the racist graffiti ever happened. But forgetting it ever happened would have put more people at risk by sending the message: "Racism will be tolerated at this school, so pollute away." Sometimes, like in this case, we have to dive in to help. Sometimes there's no way to avoid splashing crap all over the place—or at least, to avoid calling attention to the crap that's already there. So, while it would make things easier if we robot-ed a simple set of instructions at you—never do this online, always do that online, *beep boop boop*—we can't. One of the main things we've learned from our work is that life online is more complicated than *always* and *never*.

There are, however, *better* choices, more strategic choices. We can start making these choices by understanding how the winds of social media shape our online experiences and how we personally fit within the landscape. That was the focus of the last two chapters. This chapter explores the energies we're putting out into the world and what we can do to make sure we're using that energy as ecologically as possible.

Biomass pyramids illustrate how this works. Like food chains, they help explain who's eating what and, therefore, who's being *energized* by what. But it's what they help us visualize that makes biomass pyramids so helpful in conversations about social media.

Like all pyramids, biomass pyramids have a wide foundation

narrowing to a point. The herbivore layer is widest because the overall number and total weight of herbivores is highest. There are fewer secondary predators, and together they weigh less than all the herbivores. So they're the next layer up. You've probably seen something similar in your own neighborhoods or while camping. There are a ton more squirrels running around than foxes.

Because their numbers are fewest, and because they get their energy from every level below them, apex predators are at the top of the pyramid; they rule the ecosystem. But they also reveal something important: all animals, regardless of where they fit on the pyramid, are interconnected. How long top predators live and how many offspring they can produce depends on the success of their prey, which depends on the success of their prey's prey, and so on. Everybody's success, in turn, depends on the success of the ecosystem as a whole, which includes how much it rains, how healthy the soil is, and whether the animals have a sustainable habitat. Trouble for one part of the pyramid means trouble for all the rest.

You see similar relationships on social media. The most obvious sources of pollution are the people at the top of the pyramid: the on-purpose offenders (and note that the word *offenders* refers both to the harmful actions they take and to the fact that they are often quite offensive). It can, of course, be tricky to know a person's true motives online. But when you're talking about sustained patterns of harm, even Poe's Law packs up its briefcase and types out a resignation letter that reads, *You keep doing the same terrible things with the same terrible consequences over and over. You're on your own.* These offenders often cause harm and spread falsehood for financial gain, but also to amass power and control. In comparison to other types of social media users, there aren't very many on-purpose offenders—and thank goodness for that—but they can do major damage.

Just below the on-purpose offenders are oblivious offenders, people who are especially zoomed in with their humor, meme sharing, and criticisms—and who are also especially focused on making themselves visible within the ecosystem through likes, shares, and other forms of engagement. They might not set out to actively harm others, at least not the people they care about and agree with, but they can still have pretty sharp teeth by ignoring the consequences of their sharing and focusing instead on their own enjoyment, rightness, or self-branding.

Beneath the oblivious offenders is the base of the pyramid, which represents the low-key inhabitants: people who have zero intent to harm and who may even be trying to help others by posting informative videos, commenting on what others post, and discussing the day's biggest stories. Low-key inhabitants are still active online but are more likely to respond to things they encounter than be creator/influencer-types themselves. Of all the three groups, they're the least aggressive. They're also the group most likely to deny—or even take offense at the suggestion—that their actions cause harm online. In our classes, the majority of students tend to be low-key inhabitants, about a quarter are oblivious offenders, and from time to time there's an on-purpose offender or two, who, interestingly, tend to be quite polite in person.

There are important differences among on-purpose offenders, oblivious offenders, and low-key inhabitants. At the same time, just as you see offline, what happens within one layer impacts all the others. Low-key inhabitants posting videos, commenting on what others post, or chatting with friends generate enormous amounts of attention and, therefore, enormous amounts of energy within the ecosystem that oblivious offenders and on-purpose offenders feed off. This isn't a one-way energy chain, though; offenders of both stripes also generate energy by creating content that low-key users engage with—even if they're responding with a stupefied KLSDJFKJKSDK-FJHSKJ keyboard smash.

Regardless of their position on the pyramid, everyone energizes the wider ecosystem by generating data for social media platforms. The ecosystem takes all that data and directs it back into the networks. This ensures that even more people have even more things to influence, post, and comment on. And the cycle continues.

Within such a connected environment, "Who, or what, are you energizing?" is a guiding question for sharing information strategically. The following three strategies are based on this question and will help you make sure that what you put out there does the most good for the environment.

Minimize the Energy You Give to On-Purpose Offenders

Here's an example to get started:

The whole school was talking about the racist graffiti on Sara's locker. Norah, one of Sara's best friends and a reporter for the student newspaper, decided to write an article about it. She didn't want to focus only on this specific graffiti, though; the ketchup swastika incident was too similar to ignore, and besides that, there was all kinds of racist bullying and harassment happening that the school needed to do something about. She decided to talk to Orin and Kyle, since everybody knew they were behind the ketchup swastikas. Plus, they were basically professional bullies.

Both denied writing the racist message on Sara's locker, but they did have lots to say about bullying and how it didn't really count if it happened on the internet. Or in ketchup, Kyle said, which made Orin laugh. Norah asked if she could quote them in her article, and they said sure, they had nothing to hide. She also did a bunch of research on the psychology of racist bullying and how social media make the problem so much worse.

After Norah finished her article, she was excited to show it to Sara. But as they sat together so Sara could read it, Norah saw Sara's face scrunch up.

"What's wrong?" Norah asked.

"I thought you were writing an article about racist bullying," Sara said.

"I did," Norah answered, confused.

"No, this is an article about racist bullies," Sara said. "Those are two different things."

The storm of bullying at Sara and Norah's school had many social and technological causes. The focus of Norah's article gave the issue more fuel. This was good in some ways; it highlighted an important problem. In other ways, it allowed for more pollution to be sucked into the storm.

Before we talk about Norah's newspaper article, we need to underline, add an exclamation point to, and hang twinkle lights on a critical lesson from the biomass pyramid, which we hinted at earlier. The people who choose to attack and bully and spread lies online—the on-purpose offenders—do lots of damage and can wield a great deal of power over others. At the same time, they're uniquely needy within the ecosystem—more than the oblivious offenders and much more than the low-key inhabitants. Everyone is interdependent on social media. But on-purpose offenders are totally dependent on everyone and everything else for fuel.

First, without the four *A*s of social media, they'd starve. Affordances allow on-purpose offenders to take things out of context and turn them into weapons. The attention economy rewards them with, well, attention, giving them every reason to keep doing what they're doing. Once they have that attention, algorithms help spread their messages to new audiences. Assumptions that good information will always triumph over bad information, and that the worst thing you can do is restrict someone's freedom to be terrible, send the message: "Welp, what a bummer; there's nothing we can do." This hands a permission slip to on-purpose offenders to keep harming. If nobody is trying to make them stop, why would they?

On-purpose offenders are needy in other ways too. They need the likes and shares and comments and overall reactions from the pyramid's lower layers. This is because, as we mentioned before, there actually aren't that many of them. More than that, even the worst on-purpose offenders have a limited reach when it's just them talking. Without network signal-boosting, and without so many people doing their dirty work, they're just a random person standing alone on a street corner. Understanding how much on-purpose offenders depend on everybody else's resources is the first step toward minimizing their harms. We can take steps to ensure that they're fed less energy.

This idea *seems* to line up with something we've both heard a million times: "Don't feed the trolls." Or put another way, if you just ignore the person doing the harmful thing, that will make them stop. This might seem like good advice, but there are a few problems with it. One is that it blames the victim: it suggests that it's the target's fault for "letting" something bad happen to them. "If only you didn't feed the trolls," the finger-wagging goes, "then you wouldn't feel so bad right now. If you don't want to feel bad again, adjust *your* behavior." The true reason you feel bad, though, isn't because of what you did. It's because of what the person who harmed you did.

Even worse, "Don't feed the trolls" frames the problem solely in terms of individual people and individual harms. These conversations end up way smaller than they should be, because they sidestep why the behaviors are so common. Especially when the harms in question are racist or sexist or bigoted in other ways, zooming in on specific offenders tends to overlook all the supports that allow people like that to keep doing things like that. White supremacy, for example, isn't some astonishing and rare belief embraced by only a few violent freaks. White supremacy is a widespread problem that lives in economics, politics, and the legal system; we just see extreme versions of it in specific behaviors on social media. People lose sight of how big the problems are, and how much work needs to be done, if they think that not responding to this or that white supremacist troll online will somehow fix things.

For all these reasons, the advice "Don't feed the trolls" is unhelpful at best. A much more ecological approach is to ask how you can make the landscape less hospitable for these kinds of offenders. One way to do this is to say, "Nope, I'm not doing any work for you. Go home." Initially you might think, "Do work for on-purpose offenders? I would never!" And maybe you'd never do work for them deliberately. But remember, the worst offenders benefit when other people spread their messages, even if that spread is through criticism or angry pushback. They absolutely deserve criticism and pushback. That still doesn't change the fact that it helps them.

So when considering how to respond, don't just repeat the messages that on-purpose offenders post, and don't spend too much time focusing on their motives and experiences. They will certainly want the opportunity to explain themselves, since that lets them tell the story in the way they want to—typically to offer excuses for what they've done or whine about how it's someone else's fault. That's a trick, however. What matters is what impact their actions have, not what they personally think about those actions. Focus instead on the bigger stories you can tell about them: why they exist, what has energized them, and what the consequences of their actions are, rather than the basic fact that they're jumping up and down, begging for you to pay attention to them.

And that brings us back to Norah's newspaper article. There, she centered the people causing harm and even gave Orin and Kyle, well-known bullies and racist-message scrawlers, the opportunity to explain themselves. They became the stars of the show. This made Sara feel small, but it probably made Orin and

Kyle—and whoever left the racist graffiti on Sara's locker, if Orin and Kyle were telling the truth—feel pretty important.

Maximize the Energy You Give to People Who Have Been Harmed

Here's another story to set the scene:

Jake first heard about the racist graffiti from Clint, who'd found it while walking to the restroom during class. Clint texted Jake about what he'd seen but said he didn't know whose locker it was. Jake had a bad feeling and asked to be excused too. Sure enough, the locker was Sara's. He took a picture just before one of the custodians and Principal Smith stomped down the hallway, apparently looking for the graffiti. Smith spotted it, glared at Jake, and told him to leave.

Jake was sure they were going to scrub the message off and pretend the whole thing never happened, just like they did with the ketchup swastikas, so he decided to post the picture to Instagram. He tagged Sara, the school, the parent-teacher association, and everyone he could think of. He was furious! Lots of people started responding and saying how terrible the message was and demanding that Principal Smith start an investigation. Even the local paper posted something about it. Jake watched all the likes and shares roll in and was glad that he was able to help his friend.

Later that night, he texted Sara to see how she was feeling, and it took her a long time to respond. When she finally did, she said she wished he hadn't tagged her in his post, because all day she'd been getting racist messages. Many included the picture Jake took. She thought she might need to delete her account now because her parents were so worried. Even her mom had started getting nasty emails from people.

Even though he was trying to help, Jake's photo impacted the online environment in significant—and for Sara and her family, quite harmful—ways.

As we just discussed, one strategy for minimizing the energy you're giving on-purpose offenders is to shift attention away from *them* and toward the rest of the ecosystem. A good place to focus that energy is the people they have harmed, whose voices are often drowned out when everyone is tripping all over themselves to say more things about the meanest person in the room.

Especially when the targeted person is Black, Indigenous, or a person of color, it's extremely important that their experiences don't become fuzzy, abstract, and easy (for some people) to shrug off. It's also extremely important that they don't end up a side character in the on-purpose offender's drama—especially when the on-purpose offender is white and therefore tends to be the center of most stories anyway. Giving attention to targeted people also helps highlight widespread patterns: things that aren't just happening to one person but threaten entire communities. For justice to be possible, there needs to be a clear understanding of what the injustices are.

But, as always, there are risks here too. The first risk has to do with the winds of social media. When you share a story or post a comment about someone who's been harmed, you can never be sure what audiences will see it or what they might end up doing in response. Here's where Poe's Law reenters the scene, sharing spaghetti, *Lady and the Tramp*–style, with context collapse. For some audiences, your sharing might be helpful. It could inform, show support, and minimize the on-purpose offender in the story. That's good!

But for other audiences, like in Sara's story, your sharing could do something else entirely, looping us back to how even facts can pollute. Sharing could force someone to relive trauma by making them see the same harms over and over. It could put an even larger target on a person or group, setting them up for worse abuse. It could encourage the on-purpose offender, or some *other* on-purpose offender, to do something even nastier next time, since they're still getting a reaction.

Sharing stories about harm can be risky in another way, especially when the person sharing the story is not someone who has been marginalized because of their race, gender identity, ability, or difficult life experiences. Without question, it's important to show support for those who have been targeted. At the same time, the trauma experienced by marginalized groups is not a possession for people like Jake to do whatever they want with. It's not content for their social media feed. It's not a chance to show off white-person heroism. People who approach others' trauma in this way might have the best intentions and might sincerely want to help. But they can still cause harm—even if it looks very different from direct attacks.

Debra Walker King, an African American studies professor, explains how this can happen to Black people when their lives are reduced to a series of "consumable agonies." *Consumable* literally means "able to be consumed," like an object you can buy, own, or sell. *Agonies* are things that cause pain: the violence a person experiences, the ugly messages they receive, and the fear they live in. If all you're doing is showing someone's pain without any consideration to what that person thinks, feels, or wants, and without acknowledging the things that bring them joy, you reduce the wholeness of that person to one of their smaller parts. That's classic zoomed-in thinking. As always, zoomed-in thinking is the opposite of ecological thinking; it blocks perspective, and blocked perspective increases pollution risks.

So when you can, check with the person whose story it is before you share details or jump into a discussion—anything that will make their experiences more visible to more people. They might not want their story publicized, or they might have an opinion about how they want it to be shared. Just because you feel bad and want to say something doesn't mean that they're feeling the same way or want the same things.

Jake's best intentions went horribly wrong for Sara because he didn't reflect on this possibility; he was too zoomed in. In many ways, he was doing the right thing. He wanted to call attention to the racist and unjust attack that Sara experienced. He also wanted to make sure the school couldn't pretend it hadn't happened. What he didn't do is check to see what Sara wanted. He could have texted her to tell her what he was planning to do and asked if she was OK with being tagged in his post. Sara could have said no, and Jake still could have posted the photo and demanded that the school respond. That way, she could have avoided the racist backlash she and her family were forced to live through.

Reflect on What Energizes You

Imagine that Sara and Jake were your classmates. How would you feel about their story? Do you think you would have joined the protests? Do you think you would have shared or commented on Jake's post?

By answering these kinds of questions, we can begin identifying something important. And that's what energizes *us*: the beliefs we have, assumptions we make, and people who influence us. No matter how actively we might think about them, these things strongly impact our actions, including what we share and how we share it. Sometimes this can be good. Other times, the things that energize us undermine our ability to think ecologically or, even worse, set us up to pollute all over the place. Understanding ourselves, in other words, is another form of environmental protection.

WE SHARE BECAUSE OF OUR BELIEFS

Often, we believe things strongly but don't entirely know why. That's because our beliefs are shaped by so much: the experiences we've had, the people we were raised by, the things we've learned from our friends, and the books, TV, and movies we've had access to. Even though it can be difficult to say "Ah, yes, this is why I believe this thing," we can see the effects of our beliefs pretty easily, especially when they sort people between good and bad, normal and weird, worth caring about and worth ignoring.

How we sort people is hugely important. It influences whose lives we value, what we notice about someone's feelings (or if we even think they have them), and what kinds of risks we're willing to take in pursuit of our own interests. For example, we might be more likely to share embarrassing GIFs when the person doing whatever amusing thing—dancing, making a funny face, falling off a trampoline—has a different skin color or body type than ours.

Whatever our beliefs might be, if we're not aware of what's motivating us, we're more likely to harm or spread pollution when we straight-up don't notice certain things, people, or consequences.

To reflect on your beliefs in a particular situation, ask yourself some gut-check questions about what you're taking for granted. Who do I think is good here and why? Who do I think is bad here and why? Who am I worried about? Who am I not worried about? How does my worry, or lack of worry, influence what I end up sharing? By asking these questions, you might decide that, yup, you're OK to share. But you might realize that, oops, you were about to kick over a bucket of toxins.

WE SHARE BECAUSE OF OUR ASSUMPTIONS

To figure out what's giving us energy, we should also consider what assumptions we're making about the world around us. We talked about assumptions when we introduced the four winds of social media in chapter 2. The people who built social media platforms made a whole gaggle of them: that the faster information traveled, the better; that bad information would always be outweighed by good information; and that the worst thing you could possibly do is take away someone's right to say whatever they want, regardless of how ugly it might be. These assumptions influenced how the platforms were designed.

But platform decision makers aren't the only people who make assumptions about information. We encounter assumptions all the time in our research, in our classrooms, and when we talk to friends and family members. The following three are especially common.

The first assumption is that *it's safe to share something as long as it's true.* As Jake learned from Sara's harassment, this assumption can result in all kinds of downstream consequences. Even the truest information can end up polluting new audiences in unexpected ways or end up being used as a weapon by those looking to cause harm. Truth is important, and at the same time, it doesn't guarantee good outcomes. So merely checking to see if something is true before you share it isn't enough.

Another common assumption people make is that *when someone else is wrong about something, you can cure them by throwing facts at them* (and that if at first you don't succeed, just say the facts louder and more condescendingly next time). The problem is, people don't always believe things because of facts. Instead, belief is often closer to a *feeling* deep down in that person's bones.

Sharing facts isn't always useless, of course. It can be helpful if the person you're talking to doesn't care what the answer is—for example, if they're asking what Arbor Day is or how far away Mars is from Earth. Sharing facts can also be helpful if the person agrees with your worldview, like if you're telling them information about the fossil fuel industry's role in the climate crisis and they already believe, first, that the climate crisis is real, and second, that human dependence on fossil fuels helped cause it. Things get tricky when your facts contradict their feelings or when they have a totally different worldview—like if you try to share the same information about the fossil fuel industry with someone who thinks the climate is just fine and that any changes happening are natural. In these cases, you can share and share and share and it might not do a thing to change that person's mind. At best, the information will float around pointlessly. At worst, it could splash onto other audiences and do who-knows-what downstream.

A third common assumption is that *when we share things online, we're neutral participants.* People who make this assumption are basically saying that they're like wildlife photographers capturing a scene from nature—bears fighting or foxes prancing or butterflies fluttering—without any influence on the outcome. Maybe some wildlife photographers actually do that; maybe the bears or the foxes or the butterflies never know the photographer is there. But even if they don't, those photographers aren't neutral. As humans, they *can't* be. Human society has shaped the land and the climate—and all its animal inhabitants—in enormous, often catastrophic ways around the globe. The result is that no human ever gets to step outside the natural environment; we're always right in the middle of it.

We can apply the same idea to our actions on social media. Someone might claim that they're just reporting the facts. They might claim that they're not actually doing anything; they're merely sharing what the troll said. This might make someone *feel* like they're a neutral participant. But that's not possible. The consequences of our actions online might be small or they might be big. But they're always something. The result is that, just like offline, there's no way to step outside the environment.

When people make these three assumptions, they're often coming from a good place. They want to help, and their assumptions point them to what seems to be most helpful. But our assumptions can be wrong, or at least might not work how we think they will. So it's important to stop and reflect on what we're assuming will happen. Running through the three assumptions described above and asking, "Am I doing that?" is a good place to start. And then take it a step further. Ask yourself what the consequences might be—for others and for yourself—if you're wrong.

WE SHARE BECAUSE OF OUR INNER CIRCLE

Our friends and family can have an enormous impact on our beliefs and assumptions. That's why it's important to consider what *their* beliefs and assumptions are, since they're likely shaping what we think about the world and about others in all kinds of ways. This influence can be very positive, very negative, or very mixed.

When we happen to disagree with them and find ourselves the odd person out in their conversations, it's pretty easy to identify what our inner circle believes and assumes; every time they make an argument, we get irritated. That irritation directs our attention to the things we feel are wrong or strange or generally opposed to how we see things.

On the other hand, if we happen to have friends and family who think a lot like we do, it can be more difficult to identify what their beliefs and assumptions might be. That's because everything they say feels natural and normal—sort of like the air we breathe, which we never question because it's always *there*. In these cases, we have to work harder to identify the arguments people are making, because they don't feel like arguments at all. They feel like the truth.

In either case, you can ask yourself questions to pinpoint others' beliefs and assumptions. Whatever the answers to these questions might be, they'll help you better understand where some of your beliefs and assumptions come from—even if they're the result of you saying, "No, I don't believe that" or "No, I won't assume that." By considering these influences, you can identify what you're likely to notice, and what you're likely to overlook, as you navigate your online spaces.

A few gut-check questions can help. Whom does this person/group trust and why? Whom does this person/group mistrust and why? What does this person/group care about protecting? What does this person/group think is normal, and what do they think is weird? Whom and what is this person/group willing to fight for? What causes this person/group to become angry? What causes this person/group to laugh?

• • •

Reflecting on beliefs, assumptions, and inner circles, as well as where energy is going to and coming from online, can help us better understand and navigate complicated issues. Consider the racist graffiti story. Because of their beliefs, assumptions, and inner circles, Sara and Jake are energized to protest. Norah is energized to write a particular newspaper article in a particular way. Principal Smith is energized to swat away Sara and Jake's concerns. Orin and Kyle are energized to be terrible and feel pretty pleased about it. Each set of choices, in turn, energizes someone or something else—for better and for worse.

The same is true for you, for both of us, and for everyone. We are all energized by powerful, if invisible, influences. We are all, also, powerful sources of energy for others, even if we never see that energy or think a single thing about it. Just like the winds of social media, it's the unseen energies that can have the greatest impact, with the most potential for spreading pollution within the social media biomass. After all, when you don't realize that your energies are pushing others toward polluted places, you can't know to stop and rethink what you're doing. And when you don't realize that you're being pushed toward polluted places by others' energies, you can't know to dig in your heels and say, "Nope, I'm not going there."

5

Accidental Harm

• • •

The last few days had been the worst of Michelle's life, and for once it wasn't her sister Stacy's fault. It was Mike's fault. No, it wasn't Mike's fault. He felt bad too and had been messaging her about the whole mess all morning. He just wanted to show what had really happened, he said. He just wanted to keep people from making stuff up. Also, Mike thought her outfit was cute. "The public had a right to know," he'd texted, which made Michelle smile, at least for a half second.

It started innocently enough. Michelle and Mike and some of his friends from another dorm decided to meet up at the first football game of the season. That seemed like a good way to meet people, which Michelle was worried about since she was from out of state and everyone else at her college had gone to high school together. At least that's how it felt—everybody with their inside jokes and six best friends. And it was only the first week of freshman year. How was that even possible?

So she'd figured that doing something extra extra out on the field would be a good way to break the ice. She'd bounced out to the fifty-yard line all "Rah-rah sports games!" even though she hates football, looked into the crowd, and waved excitedly to Mike and the rest of the group. Also to herself on the jumbotron, which she thought was a funny thing to do, like waving to everyone at the end of a Zoom call, but she couldn't help it. Everyone waved back as Mike scrambled down the bleachers. As usual, he whipped out his phone to take a video. That kid and his videos.

With great pep, the cheerleaders explained the rules of the game: You take the school spirit stick! (Translation: a baseball bat covered in pirate mascot stickers.) You spin around with your forehead on the knob! You step through the hoops! If you make it through all of them, you get a shirt! Goooo, team! Michelle grinned—what could go wrong?—and started spinning around as the crowd cheered. She was going to be so popular.

After twenty turns around, Michelle popped her head back up. She turned toward the bleachers and tried to woo-hoo at the crowd. But something was wrong; the world kept spinning. The cheerleaders slowly backed away. Right, the hoops. She had to hop over the hoops. She took a step forward. And then she puked all over the cheerleaders' pile of pom-poms.

"Our dazzle!" one of them shouted.

Somehow Michelle ended up on the edge of the field as Mike and a few others hovered over her. After that, she was in a car, and after that, her bed. It was all pretty blurry. She didn't know that Mike had posted the video until the next morning, when she was scrolling through her feed and a bunch of people were commenting on a shorter clip from

Mike's post. All it showed was her standing next to the cheer-leaders, swaying a bit, woo-hoo-ing at the crowd, and then barfing. Within a few hours, a picture from that clip—the cheerleaders' horrified faces front and center—was posted to Twitter by the school newspaper. The tweet read, "Like a flock of squawking, drunk birds, the sorority girls have returned to our fair campus." The replies were even worse.

That was when Mike panicked, he'd explained, and reposted the original video with the caption, "This is the unedited video! Learn some media literacy! Michelle's not even in a sorority lol!," which only prompted actual soror-ity girls to scream defamation. "We have rights too," one of them posted, soliciting a whole thread about the dangers of anti-sorority bias. The most popular satire account on cam-pus reposted their favorite comments, which they captioned by asking, "Did we write this?" Students, especially the ones who weren't in Greek life, thought the blatant sorority hate was hilarious and shared the post far and wide.

All the while, Michelle watched her mentions in hor-ror. And then the local news station got wind of the story. "Tonight, a viral video sparks debate about campus drink-ing," the anchor said, frowning slightly, as the producers flashed the image posted by the student newspaper.

From there, it didn't take long for her parents to find out. "We saw the news clip on Facebook," the text from her dad read. "Your mother and I are very disappointed. Stacy looks up to you. You need to take your responsibilities seriously. Love, Dad." She started typing a response. "No that was just a clip I hadn't been drinking I…" but she stopped. What was the point? Everyone had already seen the video.

In a chapter with the word *harm* in the title, you might be surprised that our opening story wasn't about cyberbullies, dangerous strangers, or people pretending to be someone else to trick you (*catfishing*, a term that honestly still confuses us). That's because we won't be talking about those kinds of harms. Not because they aren't problems, but because there are other harms that tend not to get talked about very much, or talked about at all, when all the focus goes to the most obvious harms and the on-purpose offenders who cause them.

Polluted information about Michelle spread through many interconnecting networks, making it very difficult to correct the record.

Using Michelle's spin-game story as our primary example, we'll show that even good, well-intentioned people can end up causing harm online. We hinted at this possibility last chapter when we talked about the unintended consequences of Jake's Instagram post. In this chapter, our whole focus will be how, why, and to what effects our wild, hyperconnected networks can gobble up our posts, spit them out to all kinds of unexpected places, and cause accidental harms that can be every bit as damaging as on-purpose attacks. They're just harder to identify and harder to prevent because people don't *mean* to do damage. To begin identifying and preventing these harms, we need to zoom up and away from our motives, up and away from the specific thing we're posting, and up and away from our expected audiences to consider the downstream consequences of our actions. Zooming out helps us assess pollution risks for things we haven't posted yet. It also helps us know when we need to try to detoxify something we've already put into the world.

Oh, How the Winds Blow

If you haven't guessed already, zooming out isn't an easy thing to do. Our technologies were designed to keep us zoomed in, so that's what we typically keep doing.

To set the problem up, imagine yourself on the edge of a river. You're holding a toy sailboat you just plucked out of the water. Everything right in front of you is crisp and active and bright: the shiny sailboat, the sediment in your toes, the sound and coolness of the water. You're also hyperaware of what you're thinking and feeling, including your motives for being at the shore, why you chose to grab the sailboat, and what you want to do with it next.

But side to side and behind you, there's an odd muffling; you're standing in the opening of a tent made of thick, cloudy plastic that limits your senses and overall perspective. This is the tent you know, though, and it's always been like this. So you stay focused on your sailboat.

Outside your plastic tent, there's all kinds of context and relevant data. You just can't access it, which complicates your ability to make fully informed choices. For instance, not knowing the story of how the sailboat got to you—if it was stolen, if it's a priceless antique, if it's secretly a bomb—means you can't be sure what will happen or who might get mad if you put it back in the water. Not knowing what's downstream means you can't anticipate where the boat might end up if you relaunch it, what it might do once it gets there, and how it will impact different groups along the shore, especially if the boat has radioactive paint or some other built-in danger that you're not aware of. Needless to say, these are accidental harms just waiting to happen.

This is the position we're frequently put in online. Once again, we can thank the four *A*s of social media. Building on what we've already covered, here's what each *A* ends up obscuring:

Affordances chop things up into pieces—images, GIFs, audio clips—and send those pieces zooming across different platforms and audiences. We often don't know where something came from, who made it, or the impact something has had on other people. So it's difficult to know when something is polluted or could become polluting.

The attention economy favors the loudest, most dramatic, and most extreme kinds of content and people. We often don't know about the things that are quieter, calmer, and more thoughtful—or that simply aren't trending. So it's difficult to know what else we could be doing, reading, or thinking about.

Algorithms direct attention to what we already like, believe, or want. We often don't know what we're not being shown or why algorithms are recommending *this* rather than *that*. So it's difficult to know when we have a warped, incomplete picture of something.

Assumptions about information, speech, and freedom are why affordances, the attention economy, and algorithms were designed to work as they do. We often don't know whose voices have been silenced or overamplified because of these assumptions. So it's difficult to know who needs help or what the root of certain problems are.

The question is, if we're missing so much information online, why does it feel like we're drowning in information? The answer is simple. We *are* drowning in information. The toy sailboat we're holding, the sediment beneath our feet, the water rushing by, and all our thoughts and feelings are, already, a lot to take in. It's easy to assume we know everything there is to know. But the world is always so much bigger than our own personal hideouts.

Kicking Up All Kinds of Accidental Harms

Online, there are three main risks when our point of view is limited to the (metaphorical) sailboats in our hands. Each can result in harms that we're not likely to notice or worry about because, again, we don't *mean* to cause any harm. But that doesn't mean we won't.

First, when our perspective is limited on social media, we can accidentally *stomp on consent and privacy.* Consent is an incredibly important issue online and off. It means a person is fully informed of what's happening and agrees without pressure to do something. When we respect consent, we send the message "You get to choose what happens to you, and if you say *no,* that outweighs my *yes.*" We've talked about the importance of yeses and nos in earlier chapters; both are critical to maintaining healthy boundaries. Online, consent is also closely related to privacy, which is a person's right to decide how much attention they get. If a person asks for privacy but someone exposes them or gives them unwanted attention anyway, that's a consent violation; it means someone else has decided that their *yes* is more important than the other person's *no.*

When people talk about consent and privacy violations online, they often focus on the most obvious, on-purpose examples, like maliciously sharing private pictures or secrets. These behaviors can be devastating and are important to talk about. But on social media, it's very easy, and in fact very common, to strip a person of their right to choose without even realizing it. Once again, the culprit is zoomed-in thinking. We become so focused on the thing right in front of us that we forget about consequences for others and, even more basically, the fact that other people might be saying no. Here's an example from Ryan's teenage daughter Sophia that shows how this can happen (and, yes, he asked for permission to share it):

> Sophia has been using the music app Spotify for years, but until recently she had ignored its social features. She didn't have a cute profile picture or a cool screen name and followed not a soul. She was happy to exist in her own private playground where she could listen to what she wanted, when she wanted, and how she wanted, without worrying about who was keeping track. But then all her friends started sharing their Spotify accounts with each other, and suddenly she felt pressure to join in. She thought it over and decided not to tell her friends her account name; she wanted her music to be an escape and didn't want to worry about what the group chat might say every time she cued up a song.
>
> One friend of hers, though, was enterprising enough to find Sophia's account anyway. That friend shared it with the group, complimented some of Sophia's music taste, and went on with her day. Meanwhile, Sophia now found her own day derailed as she googled privacy settings and mulled over whether to just give in, pick some kawaii avatar, and open up the social media floodgates.

In this story, Sophia's friend wasn't trying to stomp on anybody's anything—the opposite, in fact. She was focused on having fun on a fun app with someone she liked, and she used the technological tools at her disposal to make that happen. But that friend didn't stop to ask Sophia if her answer was yes or no before she shared her profile with the group, even though Sophia had already signaled that she didn't want to share by not sharing when the group swapped profile names.

Consent and privacy issues also come up—and come up very, very often—when people share funny content online, a topic we'll be exploring in even more detail in the next chapter. Sometimes the "punch lines" are people: somebody's friend or mom or sister or you, transformed into a meme or GIF or screenshot. Just another set of pixels on the screen. When all you're doing is playing with pixels, you're not as likely to worry about the person behind the meme or GIF or screenshot, or how your actions might impact them, their friends, or their family. You're also not as likely to worry whether they want to be a silly joke between strangers, or if they want their face plastered across social media. So you go ahead and make those choices for them, not realizing that there are consent and privacy toes you need to avoid stomping on.

Consent, or the lack thereof, is a basic part of Michelle's spin-game story. All the editing and sharing and commenting that resulted from Mike's video obscured a basic fact: Michelle is a person who didn't want a clip of her puking into a pile of dazzle to go viral. She especially didn't want people to draw the false conclusion that she puked because she was drunk. But once the video entered her college network, Michelle-the-person was reduced to Michelle-the-viral-clip-OMG-did-you-see-it. In an instant, she became something—not even some-one—to giggle about and share with friends. For the people laughing, it was a fun and funny time. They might not have meant to, but they still took away Michelle's ability to say, "Please don't."

The people laughing at Michelle altered the online environment by commenting and sharing the video clip, making the landscape less comfortable for Michelle.

The basic tip for avoiding this outcome is to remember that every funny GIF, unflattering image, or out-of-context clip captures a moment in another person's life. They might not want to be reduced to a meme and might have all kinds of reasons to want privacy, from social anxiety to being in danger from a violent person in their life. So before you share, think of someone you love and ask yourself, How would you feel if they were the one whose *no* was being ignored?

The second accidental harm caused by limited perspective is *anger directed at the wrong people and things*. In chapter 2, we talked a bit about anger. As we explained, anger isn't always a bad thing we should avoid by default. Anger can be very good and even necessary to ecological thinking. It's a real problem, however, when people end up *misdirecting* their anger.

Chapter 2 also described how the winds of social media ensure that angry misdirection happens constantly. The winds are great at zooming us in, recommending this over that, and amplifying the loudest voices. But helping us understand why we're seeing certain things online and when we're missing context? That's not their department.

So standing comfortably in the opening of our tent, sediment beneath our toes and toy sailboat in our hands, it might seem like we have all the information we need to make smart decisions about who we're mad at and how we should react. Maybe we're wrong, though. Maybe the thing we *think* is bad because it *looks* bad isn't actually bad—or isn't bad in the ways we assume it is. Maybe we've fallen for someone else's trick.

This last point is key. For years, we've seen people fall for all kinds of tricks over and over again, which is why we encourage students and journalists alike to proceed with extreme caution when suddenly everybody seems to be mad about something on social media. On-purpose offenders love, *love*, l-o-v-e to trick people into misdirected anger—just like Orin and his goat trolls did when they pretended to get into a fight about Tabitha's TikTok.

Often they do this by making bad-faith arguments. A bad-faith argument is a dishonest argument; at least one participant is lying about what they believe, or simply doesn't care what the truth is. Orin was acting in bad faith when he posted what Neev said about third block. Orin wasn't actually offended; Orin wanted other people to get offended and attack Neev, which is exactly what happened. On-purpose offenders also stir the social media pot by creating fake accounts (sometimes called "sock puppets") and impersonating real people to generate publicity, engagement, and anger at something that's totally made up.

These examples are extreme (though not uncommon). But regardless of the cause—whether it's the result of active trickery or the winds of social media blowing everybody off course—when we're wrong about what we're angry about, we can cause all kinds of harms without realizing it. For the person or group who ends up targeted, this can be equally scary and confusing—not to mention unfair. Consider what happened to Michelle. The people who saw Mike's video thought they knew what it was: a drunk sorority girl, or at least a student who was making the college look bad. In response, they lashed out. But they had their facts wrong. Same thing for all the people yelling at Mike's correction (and all the people who couldn't stop laughing at the sorority girls' anger). Based on the details of the story, there's no reason to think that anybody was trying to set Michelle up or actively hurt her. That, of course, made zero difference to Michelle, who still had to figure out how to respond to her disappointed dad.

Technological and social forces blew Mike's video all over the internet, picking up and dumping out more and more pollution as it traveled.

Because of all these question marks, the tip for avoiding accidental harm is to ask what you don't know about what you're seeing online. Do you know what the poster's or sharer's motives are? Do you know how many people are participating? Do you know how many of the accounts are connected to actual people and how many are fake? How does not knowing this information impact your ability to think about downstream consequences? Who or what might be harmed if it turns out you're wrong?

The third accidental harm caused by limited perspective is that it can *toxify efforts to tell the truth and help others*. Of all the consequences we've talked about, this one is the slipperiest. In our experience, it also tends to be the most common consequence of zoomed-in thinking, which is why we've highlighted the issue in several of our stories and why we need to underline the point again here. Many, *many* people assume that we can get rid of false information by saying as much true information as possible. Journalists especially rely on this idea. For example, it's standard practice for reporters to respond to hoaxes and conspiracy theories with fact checks explaining in point-by-point detail why the hoax or conspiracy theory is false. This assumption is also common among people who are trying to set the record straight by defending someone's reputation, providing more context, or offering proof.

Without a doubt, fact-checking can be critical. And, as we mentioned last chapter, efforts to set the record straight can 100 percent be the right thing to do. Both can clarify an issue and give people the information and support they need. For certain audiences, this is ideal. For other audiences, calling attention to false and harmful information can have a very different effect. This is where the "accident" in "accidental harm" comes from. People doing the right thing, or what seems like the right thing, can actually reward on-purpose offenders by exposing even more people to information pollution, by making bad information stick around longer, or by putting people in harm's way (like how Jake's Instagram post pointed racists toward Sara's account and even toward her mother).

Whether it happens in news stories, on social media platforms, or in group chats, the assumption that facts will always help comes from a well-meaning place. If this were how things worked, though, the only rule we'd need to follow online would be to tell the whole truth and nothing but the truth every single chance we get. But alas, the winds of social media make our lives much more difficult than that by ensuring that even good information can have bad, or at least mixed, effects.

In Michelle's case, facts were a main source of harm. She became a target not because Mike lied about what happened. She became a target because Mike revealed the truth. As he explained, he thought he was doing Michelle a favor by showing what actually happened. But by "helping"—that is, posting (and then reposting) the full video—Mike accidentally ensured that the moment would live on in remixable, searchable infamy. That's what allowed someone to edit the longer clip down to the most clickable moment, capturing the attention of the school newspaper—and later, the local TV station. Mike's defense of Michelle also backfired. It was true that she wasn't a sorority girl. But by saying so, he riled up the actual sorority girls, creating more of a spectacle and more opportunities for more people to make more jokes. That narrowed people's perspectives even further. Once again, Michelle was the one who paid the price.

The tip here is to remember that just because you're trying to help online doesn't mean you will. It's also important to remember that truth can still pollute. You might be earnestly critiquing something bad. You might be laughing your head off with your friends because a false claim is so ridiculous. Downstream, those motives don't matter. All that matters is what happens next, and what happens next can be very harmful indeed.

● ● ●

The more zoomed in on the landscape we are, the easier it is to cause accidental harm. Adding to this problem, the more convinced we are that harm is only something that bad people do on purpose, the easier it is to continue doing the same accidentally harmful stuff again and again. There's just no reason to stop and say, "Wait, is this really a good idea?"

On the other hand, when we consider how the winds of social media restrict our perspective, and how a limited perspective has all kinds of murky consequences, we're able to plot out a fuller picture of the river, its surrounding land, and what to watch out for downstream. This allows us to identify possible harms as they flow past our spot.

Still, even when we're careful, we might not be able to avoid *all* harms, something we've emphasized in several of our stories. But we can avoid the avoidable ones, and so we should avoid them. The goal is to benefit other people. At the same time, *everyone* is standing downstream from someone—actually, millions of someones. Fewer harms for others means less worry for us all.

6

Online Humor and Play

• • •

It happens all the time. Something makes us fall over laughing, but then when we tell someone about it, they try to force a chuckle (maybe!) but otherwise don't react.

Here's an example. A few years ago, the two of us were flying to Brazil to give a talk. We realized that our plane had Air Chat, an instant messaging app installed on its seat-back screens, which, we reasoned, could be helpful if you needed to message a friend or family member sitting in a different row. But the app also had public forums on all kinds of hobbies and interests, which we thought was maybe less helpful. In fact, it seemed like a recipe for shenanigans.

This of course gave us an idea. Whitney for some reason chose the username "lunch," Ryan chose the equally random "Buffalo," and we started posting away. In the entirely empty Music forum, Whitney wrote simply, "i don't like it." Ryan responded by deliberately mangling his grammar and spelling. "try to lstern to others of it," he wrote. "no," Whitney wrote back. We were laughing so hard we could hardly breathe. However, there's a good chance that you, our dear reader, just kinda blinked at that story and our childish antics. So we'll say what we've said, and we're sure you've said, about humor many times before: you just had to be there.

One of the reasons humor doesn't always make sense, especially in the retelling, is that it's so tricky to pin down. Like when you start laughing about something, then can't really explain *why* when someone asks what's so funny. All you can do is repeat the funny thing.

> **RYAN:** I had that experience when we were posting to Air Chat. If the poor man sitting next to us had asked, "Why are you two giggling like cartoon characters?" all I would have been able to do is point to Whitney's last response and stutter, "She said no, about listening to MUSIC," before losing it again.

Things get even stranger when you think something is funny but you don't laugh, even if you respond by typing out an "lol," or when something is totally *un*funny, or even terrible, and you burst out laughing.

> **WHITNEY:** Like how the other night as I was innocently making coffee for the following morning, I started pouring out the old coffee and THERE WAS A DEAD MOUSE INSIDE THE CARAFE. I FaceTimed my mom to show her, and she immediately burst out laughing. I texted another friend for moral support, and she started laughing too. Then I texted Ryan, who was too grossed out to speak as I stood there cackling because I felt so horrified and sad about the mouse.

Even figuring out what counts as humor can be difficult. First, lots of jokes aren't funny.

RYAN: Just ask my kids. Like so many dads, I deliberately make bad puns at them. Unlike a lot of dads, though, when they stare at me blankly in response, I just stare dead-eyed right back. I then say, "Wocka wocka" with absolutely no inflection, like a horror movie Fozzie Bear, and go on eating my cereal.

Another complication is that lots of things that aren't meant to be funny end up being very funny indeed.

WHITNEY: Just ask my family, since we laugh and laugh at the most random things. Like a few years ago when my mom and I were walking through a furniture store and saw an inspirational wall sign that read, "Let whatever you do today be enough," except the cursive font used for the word *enough* looked like *menugh*. That made us laugh for twenty minutes. We left the store but kept laughing about menugh. The next day, we drove the half hour back to the store so my mom could get me the sign as a birthday present. It's now hanging in my office.

In these and so many other cases, humor can't be classified very easily; often, we know it when we feel it but don't have much more to say than that.

The "this is funny" feeling is what we'll be focusing on in this chapter, whether or not people actually laugh, whether or not something is meant to be funny, and whether or not something is a straightforward joke. That, of course, covers a whole lot of ground; so much of what we encounter on social media lines up with the "this is funny" feeling, at least it does for someone. To think ecologically, we need to better understand how that feeling works and what its consequences can be. That's because humor isn't a thing that only *happens* to happen online. Humor on the internet is often a very unique product of the internet. That can be great! LOL forever.

At the same time, all the winds that make so many things so amusing online can also make humor go terribly, horribly wrong. Now, some people have that intention from the outset. They use humor as an excuse to attack others and then, as soon as someone takes offense, spin around and shout that they were just joking or just trolling—when, in fact, causing offense was their goal in the first place. They just didn't want to take responsibility for what they were saying (looking at you, Orin and Kyle). We're not talking about that kind of humor in this chapter, which we'd lump into the on-purpose offender category of the biomass pyramid.

Instead, we're considering humor that's meant to be fun and funny, but which can do something much less fun—such as making people angry or triggering pollution chain reactions—once it travels downstream. To echo some of the lessons from last chapter, learning about the accidental effects of even well-meaning humor helps prepare us to enjoy the best of it and avoid its most polluted runoff. Funnily enough, taking an ecological approach to humor can also help make us seem funnier to others—because our jokes are more likely to make people laugh and are less likely to splash them with toxins.

LMAOing Offline

Before we can dive into a discussion of humor online, we need to explain how humor works offline. That way we can isolate what makes humor on social media different and, beyond that, how the online environment sets us up to pollute in ways that simply aren't possible offline. To show how, we're revisiting Whitney's cup-throwing incident from the introduction.

As a reminder, her parents and younger brother and sister were visiting her at college in Northern California in 2003. They took a day trip to a nature attraction we're calling Redwood Adventure Park and were having a grand (and also pretty weird and funny) time. At one point, Whitney's sister handed an empty hot-chocolate cup to their mom, who proceeded to throw the cup on the ground. This moment shows all that goes on when a group of people think something is funny. Spoiler alert: it's a lot.

REFLECTION Do you have any classic family inside jokes? If so, consider how each of these points connect to those stories. If your family isn't especially jokey, substitute jokey (offline) stories between you and your friends.

First, *humor signals "This is play,"* or to put it another way, "OK, I'm joking now." Sometimes these signals are communicated through words ("Did I tell you the story about [whatever]? You'll die"), but often it's through tone of voice or body language. Both kinds of signals create what scholar Gregory Bateson calls a **play frame**, where participants enter into an unspoken agreement: whatever is happening, and whatever is said, doesn't mean what it would mean outside the play frame, like when friends say rude things to each other and know it's a sign of affection rather than an actual attack (or when dogs play-bite each other and their tails keep wagging, which is the example Bateson uses). That's when the play frame *works*. When it doesn't, a person takes the humor seriously and, as a result, can have their feelings seriously hurt.

WHITNEY'S FAMILY-FUN HOT TAKE: My mom's cup-throwing shocked us because, initially, we weren't aware of the play frame. She was totally deadpan. Once she started laughing, though, we saw that she'd been playing and then were able to laugh along with her—because suddenly we all were in on the joke.

Second, *humor creates social groups* by connecting people through their laughter; it makes them closer in the moment and can help strengthen relationships over time.

WHITNEY'S FAMILY-FUN HOT TAKE: The best memories I have with my family are about the weird stuff we've laughed at. It's not just fun, though. It's why we're close. Basically, I'm related to my family because of blood, but I'm friends with my family because of humor.

Third, as fun as it can be to laugh within a group, *humor creates outsiders* by dividing the laughing *us* from a non-laughing *them*. Maybe the non-laughing *them* "only" ends up feeling left out. Maybe they're the target of the laughter. Maybe they become a target when they don't laugh.

WHITNEY'S FAMILY-FUN HOT TAKE: Now, not everybody gets Phillips family humor. It's extremely absurdist, for one thing. It's also extremely irreverent. And it's one inside joke after the other. A very sincere, very reverent person who has never heard any of our stories would almost certainly feel out of place if they were suddenly transported into the middle of a family event. At the very least, they probably wouldn't find our jokes very funny.

So, the mere act of using Phillips family humor around outsiders could create a confused, non-laughing *them* to our silly, giggling *us*. In the cup-throwing case, we created another *them*: anyone who saw my mom throw the cup but didn't stick around long enough to see us start laughing. My mom wasn't trying to make anyone uncomfortable, but I'll admit, the idea that strangers—*them*—could have seen her toss the cup and then get mad about her littering was part of what made the whole thing so funny.

Fourth, *humor emerges from clash-that-makes-sense.* A major reason people think something is funny is because things that otherwise don't belong together—words or images or situations—have collided. Folklorist Elliott Oring explains that this clash can't be too random or too extreme. It needs to be "just right" to make sense within a particular culture, which could be as large as a nation or as small as a friend group. A person who doesn't understand that culture is less likely to understand the clash and, therefore, is less likely to understand the humor. So for humor to work—or even be recognized as humor—the audience needs to be on the same basic cultural page as the person who shares it.

WHITNEY'S FAMILY-FUN HOT TAKE: There were a bunch of clashes-that-made-sense in this case. First, as a rule, my mom doesn't just throw trash around. So seeing her do something so out of character was automatically pretty funny. Second, my sister had been minding her own business (though she was, apparently, thinking of my mom as a walking trash can), which made the sudden act of cup violence so surprising—and in turn, so funny, because we never saw it coming. Finally, when you're in a public park, you're expected to behave in certain ways. Namely, don't randomly Oscar the Grouch all over the grounds. Seeing my mom stomp on those expectations made us laugh.

Fifth, *humor snowballs*. Once people start making jokes together, they tend to keep making more and more, like a snowball that grows as it rolls down a hill. As the snowball rolls, old jokes mix with new jokes.

WHITNEY'S FAMILY-FUN HOT TAKE: Part of the reason the cup-throwing moment was so funny was because of all the other funny things that happened that day. Like when an employee on the adventure trail started telling us how he'd recently seen Bigfoot and her babies and that they all smelled like urine. We were already primed for laughter when Mom threw the cup. The mood continued as the day went on, including the moment at the top of the ridge when a very bored employee wearing head-to-toe pink camouflage explained, with a dramatic flourish and monotone delivery, that on one side of the platform there was the ocean, and on the other, the Awesomeness (more trees).

Thanks to our dog, Sophie, the joke-tangle kept growing even after we left. Not only did Sophie roll around in a dead crab on the way back to Cal Poly Humboldt, stinking up the car for the rest of the weekend, but she also peed all over my parents' bed in the hotel room that night. When we start telling one of those stories now, we end up telling them all.

Sixth, *humor is magnetic*. When people laugh about something, it often attracts the attention of those outside the group. Maybe they end up laughing too. Maybe they don't, and instead end up mad. In either case, the humor sucks in more people.

WHITNEY'S FAMILY-FUN HOT TAKE: Over the years, we've told the Redwood Adventure Park story many times to many family friends, who have subsequently been drawn into the laughing *us*. When we all get together and start telling stories, a friend who wasn't even there is just as likely to bring up the Awesomeness as a family member who was.

Finally, *humor is ambivalent*. The root meaning of the word *ambivalent* is "on both sides." It happens when an action or feeling is simultaneously one thing and an opposing thing. For example, if you love eating ice cream but also hate it because it hurts your stomach, your relationship to ice cream is ambivalent. Humor is ambivalent because it can be social and fun for the laughing *us* and, at the same time, antisocial and hurtful to the non-laughing *them*.

WHITNEY'S FAMILY-FUN HOT TAKE: My mom's cup-throwing, and all the other humor that snowballed from it, was pretty lighthearted. So the ambivalence was mild. But it was still there. We sure were having fun, and it was definitely a bonding experience. At the same time, our laughter could have seemed disrespectful to other Redwood Adventure Park visitors and employees (and it kind of was). Our laughter also made several of the workers the butts of our jokes, including Bigfoot guy and Awesomeness lady, who were just doing their jobs and were probably reciting scripts their bosses had assigned.

You may be able to guess where we're going here, since even in this low-stakes case, ethical complications are already starting to creep in. Online, things get a lot more complicated with a lot more opportunity for low-stakes humor to transform into high-stakes pollution.

The Tricky World of Humor Online

Humor online and humor offline line up in many ways. Online humor signals "This is play" using all kinds of digital winks. On video chat, these winks can include actual winks. When we're texting or posting, the winks aren't always so literal. Still, emoji, images, jokey misspellings, and a whole range of silliness help people know we don't *really* mean what we're saying. Online humor also builds social groups and, at the same time, can create serious *us/them* divides.

Whether they're big or small, and whatever our motivations might be, our actions impact the online environment. This includes creating a left-out *them* through our posts and laughter.

Online humor works because of clashes-that-makes-sense, and it fails when audiences aren't on the same page about what makes sense to clash with what. Especially when it's of the meme-y variety, online humor definitely snowballs, as one funny image can inspire a hundred remixes. All the resulting eyeballs and sharing and play is the definition of magnetic;

humor online sure draws a crowd. Here's another example of the wild world of teen humor, courtesy of Ryan's daughter:

Sophia has a running joke with her friends where they continually add names and details to their phone contacts for each other as the inside jokes pile up. To one of her friends, Sophia's number is saved as "Goatphia Blur Inigo Montoya Bone Croncher the First, May She Roast In Hell." That last part made me raise an eyebrow, but she assures me it's based on a legitimate reference and is all in good fun. (Update: When I asked Sophia if I could include this example in the book, she informed me that her friend now has her saved as just "Bubbles," offering no further explanation.)

These names are obviously absurd, but the clash makes sense within Sophia's social circle. This is a good example of humor being cultural too, because Ryan, who is not a member of his daughter's friend group, initially and incorrectly worried that Sophia's friends were being mean to one another. These names also link the friends together through their humor, which keeps snowballing. And it attracts attention when other friends see messages come in from Goatphia Blur Inigo Montoya Bone Croncher the First, May She Roast In Hell (or Bubbles, apparently), and they want to know who, what, and why. This is certainly fun for the inner circle of friends, but it transforms anyone who doesn't have a jokey name into a *them*, potentially making those other friends feel left out.

Despite all the similarities between online and offline humor, there are also important differences. We saw this earlier in the book when we time-machined the Redwood Adventure Park cup-throwing story into the social media era. It wasn't difficult to imagine how Phillips family humor back in 2003 would have looked different and had different effects two decades later. We have the four *A*s of social media to thank for that.

Affordances play the most obvious role. The ability to slice and dice media into smaller, more easily post-able (and, very often, more easily mockable) pieces, to search for funny things, and to save those things for later create nonstop material for humor. The result is that there's a million little punch lines, or potential punch lines, flying around.

Platform design also creates the perfect conditions for humor. Specifically, our social feeds jumble all kinds of things together by positioning this unrelated thing alongside that unrelated thing. Much of the content people post is funny, or trying to be funny, thanks to the ability to play with LOLable images or clips or memes. But even when content isn't funny in and of itself, the random clash between posts can create a clash-that-makes-sense when this thing and that thing are stacked on top of each other. As a result, our feeds often feel funnier than they would if we were looking at the posts separately.

Once humor is afoot, affordances collide with the attention economy, algorithms, and assumptions to help spread it. The attention economy selects for the most popular and very often the most shocking or offensive humor. Algorithms push trending jokes and memes to the tops of people's feeds. And assumptions about information ensure that even the meanest humor is allowed or even encouraged to spread.

At least, this is what the four *A*s *can* do. Even with the strongest gusts, not all humor goes viral (ask anyone who crafts the

Perfect Funny TikTok or the Perfect Funny Tweet and then has their soul crushed when the likes don't come pouring in). What these four winds definitely do, however, is create the potential for humor to blow from this audience to that audience and end up being in a million places at once. Obviously, humor spreads offline too, but nothing like this. People need to actually know each other to share jokes offline, which limits how far and how fast offline humor is able to travel. Online, knowing somebody isn't necessary to finding their humor, and knowing you isn't necessary to them finding yours.

Digitally Mediated Uh-Oh

The winds of social media are humor generators. They're also why online humor can have such far-reaching consequences. It doesn't take much at all, maybe a single share from a single person, for things to go from a fun and funny "This is play" place to a toxic place. Or at least to an ambivalent place, as the following examples illustrate.

Sara and Black-Lady GIFs

The meme started after we got an email from the school about poison mold in the air vents. They had to close school for a week while they cleaned it up. Of course everyone started posting to the group chat and joking. Clint posted a bunch of celebration GIFs, and the last was of a Black lady marching out onstage saying HERE I AM, WORLD. That was definitely a good GIF, but then everybody else started posting GIFs of Black ladies dancing around, making faces and being dramatic. After that, the joke was to post a Black lady pretty much whenever anybody said anything. As if just seeing a Black lady suddenly made everything hilarious.

I didn't want to say anything because they just added me to the chat. But when my mom was looking over my shoulder and saw all these Black-lady GIFs, she asked why they were doing that. I said I didn't know. She asked if they ever posted a million GIFs of white ladies acting up and I said no. She asked if they ever posted a million GIFs of Black ladies having a cup of coffee or talking to somebody at work or walking their dog. I said no to that too. She shook her head and said maybe they wouldn't think Black ladies were walking punch lines if they knew any besides us.

Norah and Brother-Kidnap Jokes

My friends and I have a lot of inside jokes and one of them is the different terrible things that could happen to our brothers, like if they were kidnapped or thrown in a river. I follow all those stories already because there's one million crime YouTubes and TikToks but the actual jokes started after Aida's brother puked in her ice cream. She wasn't mad but for some reason that made us start sending each other freak accident/kidnap/murder stories like, "Here's a good idea for Benjamin" or "Have you thought about this for Jamel?" (Benjamin and Jamel are our younger brothers.)

We made a list of the best ones and posted them. So, the top ten ways to get rid of your brothers in just a few easy steps. Everybody thought the list was funny and added more links, and some of the brothers were posting, being like, well then, here's what can happen to sisters, and posting other weird death stories. Aida's mom even fake-posted as Jamel to add sister-kill ideas. Then Clint texted with a bunch of sad-face emojis. I thought he was making a joke too. Like he was pretending to be sad about a fake brother kidnap or something. So I said something brother-jokey, and he messaged, "I just found out my brother is in the hospital, he's on a breathing machine." And I felt horrible.

Fictional College Freshman Whitney and the Awesomeness

Well, so as we were driving back to the hotel and advising David on how to navigate his messy Stessy drama, I took the opportunity to post my delightful series of Awesomeness selfies. I described how the Awesomeness was basically just more trees, fashionista details about the worker's sweet pink-camo tracksuit, her inspiring words and even more inspiring delivery oh wait just kidding it made me fall asleep. And then I tagged Redwood Adventure Park so people would know I wasn't making it up lol.

By the time we got back to the hotel, my best friend Katie had posted a thing where she said on one side the ocean (her toilet), and the other the Awesomeness (her tail-wagging dog who had just been enjoying a nice refreshing drink). And then a few other people did too and I showed my family and they laughed, and then we added another one when Sophie peed on my parents' hotel bed, which of course we showed her pee puddle as the ocean and her standing there guiltily as the Awesomeness. ALL FUN AND GAMES until the next morning when THE ACTUAL AWESOMENESS LADY sent me a DM saying she was so sorry she couldn't wear a fancier outfit to work. Not everybody gets to spend their time having Mom and Dad take them on vacation so they can make fun of strangers.

Have any of your friends' group-chat jokes spread
to unexpected places or had unexpected consequences?

Maybe you've had similar experiences; maybe a misunderstanding about humor has caused hurt feelings in your own
group chat. Or maybe the consequences have been more widespread, like if the misunderstanding escaped your chat, traveled
out onto the broader internet, and did even more damage. Even
if neither thing has happened to you, we bet you know people
who have dealt with one or both or worse, and for a basic reason:
problems like this aren't an accident of social media. Problems
like this are a consequence of social media.

First, because the winds of social media cut larger things
into smaller pieces and make it difficult to see a story's full
context, so much of what happens online is zoomed in. When
people zoom in to just the funny punch line, just the meme,
just the snarky comment, they might be having lots of fun. But
they're not very likely to worry about—or even be aware of—
what caused the funny thing, or what the funny thing might
end up causing. This includes people's distress, anger, and
sadness. This is where accidental harms can be most harmful,
because nobody is thinking that harm is even a possibility.

In the "Sara and Black-Lady GIFs" story, Sara's friends
zoomed in on what they thought was funny about the Black
women in the GIFs they shared. They didn't stop to consider
what was energizing them, to gesture back to chapter 4: that
their actions drew from beliefs and assumptions about Black
women, namely that they were comedy accessories. They also

didn't reflect on how their mostly white friend group never questioned these "jokes," because they never had to. It all got to be consequence-free fun for them. This made Sara feel hurt and uncomfortable because her friends were using people who looked like her as punch lines.

The winds of social media cause another problem, which we started to explore in chapter 3. Once they start to blow, they can obliterate the meaning and motives behind someone's humor. In other words: they huff and puff and blow the play frame down. A joke might end up looking like a threat. A threat might end up looking like a joke. All people have to go on is what they can observe, and as we've shown throughout the book, observation is not confirmation on social media—especially once content starts to travel across networks.

This is Poe's Law in a nutshell, which says: don't get too comfortable, friends, because you can't be sure what something really means online, especially if you're encountering it randomly. As always, Poe's Law feeds into context collapse, which describes how unpredictable social media audiences can be. You never know who might end up finding something once you post it. And you never know what they'll think once they do.

Norah's "Brother-Kidnap Jokes" connects here too. Norah, Aida, and everyone else who laughed all knew that they were just joking. They didn't worry or even think about the people who might find the jokes upsetting—like Clint, whose brother truly was in danger, or anyone else whose brother, other family member, or friend had been harmed or killed in the same ways. Because of how information travels on social media, it's even possible that the friends and family of the victims featured in the links people posted could have seen Norah and Aida's list.

The same goes for Fictional College Freshman Whitney. She laughed her head off at the Awesomeness and wanted to share her amusement with others. She wasn't trying to hurt anyone's feelings in the process—in fact, based on the story, it's clear that she didn't think there was anyone else in the story besides her and her family. The Redwood Adventure Park employee wasn't someone with feelings to be sensitive to or someone who could see her post. She was a background object.

Because of how zoomed in humor can be on social media and how easily the "This is play" framing is lost on new audiences, the defense "I was just joking" ends up being pretty weak online. Or it simply doesn't matter. Let's say that the sibling of a kidnapped child contacted Norah to explain how upsetting her brother-kidnap post was. Norah could say that she was just joking about kidnapped brothers being funny, just as Fictional College Freshman Whitney could say that she wasn't trying to hurt the Redwood Adventure Park employee, and just as Sara's friends could say that they didn't mean to treat Blackness as a punch line.

However sincerely they were offered, these defensive explanations wouldn't take away the other person's feelings of hurt, embarrassment, or betrayal. When it comes to online humor, we might have been joking and might have meant no harm. But just because we know what we meant and we know what our motives were doesn't mean that anyone else will—or that it will change their experience. If someone is hurt by our humor, we shouldn't assume that the problem is them: that they just didn't get our joke or are being oversensitive. We should ask what our jokes ended up doing and, further, whether the other person had any way of knowing that we *were* joking thanks to the winds of social media blowing our joke clean out of the play frame.

When these sorts of problems emerge, the ecological metaphors from chapter 3 can help cultivate better and more sensitive conversations about what happened—and prevent, or at least help clean up, pollution chain reactions in the process. The redwoods metaphor can help people explain how, where, and to what audiences something spread. The hurricane metaphor can help people consider all the energies causing the problem and what about it felt polluted or polluting. The land cultivation metaphor can help people explain what their motives were compared to what actually happened.

What these conversations reveal is something more complicated than merely shouting, "I was just joking" at someone, with the other person shouting back, "No, you weren't." When we're talking about deliberate racism, sexism, and other kinds of violent attacks disguised as humor, "No, you weren't" is the correct response. But, again, that's not the kind of humor we're talking about here. When nobody sets out to harm anyone, both things can be true: that something was said within a play frame, and that the play frame disappeared and made someone else feel bad.

The play frame doesn't always disappear on social media. Many things start out funny and stay funny and everybody has a great time. But as we said earlier, it doesn't take much to trigger a chain reaction of zoomed-in ambivalence. It can be impossible to know when that will happen. That said, when you're aware of how humor is tangled up in the online environment—and how you yourself are also tangled up in that environment—you're in a better position to think ecologically about what you're seeing and posting, helping you minimize humor's toxic potential.

To help you reflect in this way, you can ask yourself a few gut-check questions. Are you sure this is play? Are you sure this isn't play? Who isn't laughing? What is the humor doing and how is it making them feel?

Man Bun Dot Com

The takeaway from all of this is that humor online can be very tricky. We've studied it for years, and it is for us too! Here's an example from Ryan's life, which connects to everything we've talked about in this chapter. In the story, Ryan is describing an interview he did for a cable news segment about internet memes and the stock market. At the time, he had very long hair, which he would often tie up in a bun. This story was transcribed from a voice memo, which is how we talk to each other when we're too tired to write things in chat.

So I did that CNBC interview about a month ago, if you remember? And they finally published the story on their YouTube, so I'm on their YouTube talking to CNBC about Wall Street stock memes, yay. And so I did that and it got posted and then I ended up on, you know that Twitter account, Rate My Zoom Room, or Rate My Room or whatever? Where they rate people's Zoom backgrounds and it has like a half million followers and they say nice and mean things about people's Zoom room backgrounds and then give them a score? So I ended up on that, I don't know how, and I got tagged in it, right, so whoever runs this thing like scours YouTube videos and cable news appearances and then finds them on Twitter and tags them with the rating. I got an eight out of ten. They said I needed a little more art above my fireplace. Fair enough, it's stone so it's hard to hang anything on it. I've tried.

So that happened, and it was on there, and I woke up to it. And there were a bunch of likes and whatever, and some comments. One said, "Deduction for the man bun" or something like that. And another said, "Man bun violation." I looked at their profiles and they aren't like troll accounts or trying to be terror monsters; they just felt empowered to make fun of a stranger's hair in a post that the stranger was tagged in, just because it came across their feed and was funny, right?

And so I muted the thread, because I didn't need to hear any more about what people thought about my Rate My Zoom Room. Or my hair. And like, what if I was having a bad day? What if I was feeling really low about myself already? It's also funny because I have a haircut appointment in a few weeks, and I've been thinking about cutting it anyway, like over the last few weeks since I made that stylist appointment. I've just been like, yeah, it's a pain, and it's hot here, and I don't want to go into summer with it, and I'd like my hair a little shorter. So I was like, I don't know, maybe I'll just cut it off. And now I'm like, but I can't. Because these two strangers on Twitter made fun of it, so now I gotta keep it.

First, here are Ryan's answers to the gut-check questions that ended the last section:

Was this play?
It was for the people posting about my hair, I guess, though I wasn't having much fun, and I certainly didn't laugh.

What was the humor doing?

Mostly reducing me to the butt of a joke I didn't want any part of. Like, talk about my bun if you think it's so hilarious, but maybe keep me out of the conversation? I didn't ask to be @ mentioned by that account, and I didn't ask for people to tag me in their style tips.

The concepts we've talked about can help us dive in even deeper. The Rate My Room Twitter account, along with the man-bun police, signaled "This is play" through snarky word choice. For these oblivious offenders, and all the offenders who enjoy posting sick burns of random strangers' Zoom backgrounds, this Twitter account creates a laughing *us*. Everyone else, including those who end up feeling insulted or generally weirded out by all this laughter, is the non-laughing *them*. Rate My Room humor snowballed over the course of the pandemic as people were forced to do TV interviews from their living rooms, creating a growing audience for Zoom-background theater criticism.

To understand how this story impacted Ryan, you have to reflect on how media, like cable news clips, are able to travel so easily online and how platform affordances like tagging allow information shared by total strangers to end up in other strangers' feeds.

The resulting Rate My Room peanut gallery was magnetic in that it attracted attention to a bunch of different things: the TV clips, the snarkiest comments, and of course the people whose rooms and appearances were being mocked. The assumptions of the two posters who commented on Ryan's bun—specifically, that men shouldn't have them—clashed with Ryan's style choices, making his hair funny to them. In this case and all the other cases where TV guests were mocked, Rate My Room humor zoomed in on details like someone's hair or decor. The Twitter account is also ambivalent in that it's fun for the people doing the mocking but potentially much less fun for the people being mocked. This ambivalence is intensified by the affordance of tagging, which allows you to rope someone into your joke without asking.

• • •

Like all the other examples from this chapter, Ryan's man-bun story shows that humor can be pretty serious business—and it's never easy to make sense of. Building those ecological muscles, bit by bit, example by example, will help you avoid spreading, turbocharging, or creating pollution. It will also help you enjoy the funniest fruits of social media with less worry that laughter for *us* will result in heartbreak—or a style crisis—for *them*.

Conclusion

We've covered a whole lot of ground in these chapters. The introduction laid out the book's main concepts: information pollution, ecological thinking, and how all flourishing is mutual (also: cup-throwing). Chapter 1 explained how information pollution is as much about how we're doing as what we're sharing. Chapter 2 explored the four *A*s of social media—affordances, the attention economy, algorithms, assumptions—and how these winds shape what we encounter, and what we *don't* encounter, online. Chapter 3 presented guiding ecological metaphors—redwood forests, hurricanes, and land cultivation—which locate you on the network map and help you be a better storyteller and listener about what you experience online. Chapter 4 described whom and what your online choices energize, and who and what energizes you (and how to use those energies wisely). Chapter 5 offered tips for avoiding accidental harms. Chapter 6 showed how the winds of social media can blow LOLs to all kinds of strange places.

Three ideas unify each chapter. First, our intentions online are much less important than the impact of our actions. Second, nobody can stand outside the online environment; we affect our networks just by being in them. And third, everyone, even the best and most kindhearted people, can contribute to information pollution. These ideas help the two of us to make more ecological choices online. We hope they help you too.

But there's a complication lurking beneath that hope, one we hinted at in the introduction and have been secretly wringing our hands about ever since. Our information landscape is polluted, without question. There are so many false and stressful and straight-up weird things slopped all over the ground, sometimes we can't even know where we're stepping. Many, many of those false and stressful and weird things were created or shared by people just going about their lives. However, individual people just going about their lives isn't why information pollution is in every nook and cranny online. The problems are economic, political, cultural. *Big*, in other words. Because individual people aren't the cause of these big problems, it's not realistic to tell them to fix things.

If we did, that would let the industrial-grade polluters—those who take advantage of our biggest problems for personal gain or profit—off the hook. This would be like saying, "Aw, it's OK all you amoral pollution factories of the world. You're just filthifying the Earth and raining down poison because it's cowabunga for business or your personal brand. No big deal, we'll clean it all up for you, and if we don't, that's on us!" Give industrial polluters a pass, and guess what they'll keep doing.

Still, the answer isn't to give up, to say, well, there's nothing we can do. Information pollution accumulates, causes stress in ourselves and others, and triggers all kinds of toxic cycles. There are things we can do and should do to minimize the pollution we're able to minimize. Reflecting on connection, consequence, and shared responsibility—the hallmarks of ecological thinking—is an excellent place to start.

The value of this kind of thinking isn't restricted to everyday choices on social media. It's a pattern of thought, a way of being in the world. The more we flex those mental muscles, the stronger they become. The stronger they become, the easier it is to apply ecological approaches to bigger efforts—including efforts to build new systems and fight back against the systems that have failed us.

In this way, ecological thinking can make big changes in the world, since the ultimate failure of our systems is that they're *not* ecological. They're zoomed in, focused on negative freedoms ("freedom from" being told what to do, not "freedom for" the group to enjoy their freedoms equally), and more concerned about the *me* than the *we*. These were the ideas social media platforms were built on. The point was to spread information as quickly as possible, to reward the most clickable content, and to bring people what they wanted the second they wanted it. If that information was polluted, if the most clickable content was toxic, if what people wanted was terrible or racist, well, something about the marketplace of ideas, mumble mumble, it's fine, the system is fine. To be fair, more people—including those working for social media platforms—are more concerned about information pollution these days. But so many of the same old assumptions about information and negative freedoms remain.

The result is a system that really, fundamentally, isn't fine. Not because it's broken, but because it's working exactly how it was designed to work, with certain communities bearing worse consequences than others. That's the problem we need to solve—and by *we*, we mean everyone, but especially young people, since soon enough you'll be inheriting the mess adults have made (sorry). To tackle these enormous challenges, we have to cultivate a new landscape entirely, to ensure that flourishing really is mutual. To ensure that we all get to be happy and safe and free.

We can't do that if we stay zoomed in—if all we notice is the stuff right in front of us, and if the only people we care about are the ones in our closest networks. We need to go on a different adventure, from the soil we tend and the crops we grow to the roots that support our tallest trees to the winds that whip and howl overhead. What we find won't always be pleasant—the fruits that have been poisoned, the trees that have been clear-cut, the changing climate that has fueled bigger and more dangerous storms. But by zooming out beyond ourselves, beyond whom we know, beyond our neighborhoods and states and countries, as the mountains grow small and the atmosphere thins, as the curve of the horizon gives way to a sphere and the Earth in its wholeness comes into our view, we're reminded of the one thing we all share: this place, our only place. Let's tend to it, and to one another, for everyone's sake.

Acknowledgments

When we decided to adapt *You Are Here*—our 2021 book published by the MIT Press—into a digital ethics guide for younger readers, we were entering uncharted creative waters. Gita Manaktala, MIT Press editorial director, never wavered in her support for the project and generously guided us to the right people at MIT Kids/MITeen and Candlewick Press. Among them, we are especially indebted to Hilary Van Dusen, who from the very start of the project was incredible to work with; she helped us develop a new facet to our collaborative voice and gave extraordinarily helpful feedback as we revised, and revised, and revised the manuscript. Candlewick's Hannah Mahoney and freelancer Susan VanHecke were fantastic to work with too; their copyedits were careful and detailed and across-the-board stellar. And Carolynn DeCillo's page design (and icon artistry) blew us away. We are so grateful.

Throughout the adaptation process, our students at the College of Charleston and Syracuse University also offered thoughtful responses and perspectives. We thank them for their focus, interest, and resilience (and ideas for case studies). We're equally grateful for the scholars who asked interesting and difficult questions about *You Are Here* following the book's publication. These exchanges pushed us to refine, reframe, and rethink elements of our argument, reflected throughout this book; in particular, Siva Vaidhyanathan helped us worry more/worry better about the tension between individual action and collective change, Claire Wardle was an amazing sounding board for discussions of the power of narrative, and Viktor

Chagas expanded our theoretical and global horizons. And a big thank-you to each other, of course.

FROM RYAN: I would like to thank Sarah, Sophia, Gabe, and Pearl for their grounding and support through this and every other project. This last year, blaring all our favorite songs from all our favorite playlists while we cleaned up after dinner was deeply important to me in deeply profound ways. A particular shout-out to Sophia for the instructions on the ins and outs of actual teen social media use, for all the stories from all your group chats, and for letting them animate this work. Your interest and deliberation made this book a unique joy to write. And thanks to Sophia's friends for the input anytime Sophia asked. Thanks to the power puppy Backpack for being my best friend who never did anything wrong and for the serotonin boost while I wrote.

Thanks to brother Eric for convincing me to buy a PlayStation and for our voice chat hangouts while we've played. You were an anchor through the fiercest gales of Hurricane COVID. So were Dave and April, who were always a text away for a movie night or game night or beach night or sushi night or any other kind of needed night. No better lockdown podmates. Thanks to mom for all the support as always. Thanks to all my friends and colleagues at the College of Charleston, who were without exception interested in this project and advocates of its importance. Not every academic feels empowered to write to younger audiences, and more of us should. I'm glad I got the chance.

Last, thanks to everyone for reading, and thanks for caring. Collective care is the only way we make it through.

FROM WHITNEY: I would like to thank my family for providing so much narrative and comedic fodder for the book: El (I'm so proud of you), Culdro, Tony, Wokie, Dum, and Wandor, I love you all so much. A big thanks also to Dad and Carol. Everett too, and Stevie. Moo, you have been a hero these last few years, and Vati, it goes without saying—but we will keep saying it—that you are a unicorn. To Anne, Mark, Wesley, Brandy, Joannie, Erik, Jesse, Chris, Lisa, Abby, Ang, and Ashley: your good cheer and variously mediated check-ins have been lifelines. Thank you to Chuck for being such an enormous source of support and care in Syracuse; I'll miss you. Same to Theresa, whose help in Syracuse (with Maple and Everett, with home and life logistics, weird emergencies) was crucial and generous and saved the day so many times. I don't know what I—or sweet Maple, or circus cow Everett—would have done without you.

Thank you to my colleagues at the University of Oregon and everyone in UO's School of Journalism and Communication. I'm writing this a few months before making the move back to Eugene, and by the time this book comes out, I'm sure there will be lots of people I will wish I'd had a chance to thank (how's that for verb tense usage?). I promise to do so early and often. For now, Carol, Michael, Seth, Regina, I'm not even in Oregon yet and I already feel at home (again). Thank you. Also: Brucce.

Kato: you are a grounding force as always. Thank you for keeping me updated on the latest Martha goings-on, for your encouraging feedback on the very first, very weird draft of this book, and for driving all the way to that park (I'm still wearing the ring I found in the trash).

Traveling south, thank you, Marty (and the various branches of the family tree, with an especially enthusiastic hat tip to Uncle Ron), Lynnika, Naomi, Maxwell, Hank, and the gang, and Benjamin, for helping make Humboldt a second home for, I don't know, the fourth time? Thank you, John, for more than you know, or maybe you already do, dear ghost. Thank you to the Cal Poly Humboldt Philosophy Department for inviting me to present parts of this book to the philosophy forum (three cheers to you, Mary!); and an even bigger thank you to the department, all those years ago, for encouraging my curiosity/bewilderment about what was beneath the assumptions that everything else was built on ("Another turtle?" I can imagine John half joking).

Finally, to Andy, North Star via lug nuts—thank you for every gentle word, every story told, every chuckle that shakes your laptop. The hawk was right about everything.

Source Notes

INTRODUCTION

p. 5 foundational account of environmental justice as it affects Black communities: Bullard and Wright.

p. 5 unequal effects of air pollution in the United States: Colmer and Shimshack.

p. 5 just by living their lives, they're at a greater risk of being poisoned: an example of environmental injustice in action from "How Uniontown, Alabama, Became Victim of Environmental Injustice."

p. 5 Pew Research study of online abuse and harassment: Vogels.

pp. 5–6 syllabus showing how disinformation (online and off) has disproportionately targeted marginalized groups: Marwick et al.

pp. 5–6 Data & Society study of online abuse and harassment: Lenhart et al.

p. 5 a study of the scale of transphobia online: Brandwatch and Ditch the Label.

p. 5 how falsehood and bias are programmed into many technologies: Buolamwini.

pp. 6–7 a panel presentation explaining how we can't tackle pressing global issues in a dysfunctional information ecosystem: Steenfadt.

p. 10 the overlap(s) between environmental and human systems: Morton.

p. 11 the overview effect and its ethical consequences: Nethery.

p. 11 video about overview effect: "Overview."

p. 11 "all flourishing is mutual": Kimmerer, 16.

CHAPTER 1

p. 18 discussion of social media fatigue and its behavioral effects: Dhir et al.

p. 18 social media fatigue and COVID information sharing: Islam et al.

p. 18 interview with journalist Karen Ho: Bushwick.

pp. 18–19 reflection on student COVID stress and social media sharing: Phillips, "To Fight COVID-19, Curb the Spread of Germs—and
Rumors."

p. 20 the brain science of overwhelm: Jha.

p. 20 stress and the lizard brain: Grimes.

p. 25 an overview of the body's response to stress: Harvard Health.

pp. 25–26 how the physical structures of our brain shape well-being:
Notebaert.

p. 26 the stress response and strategies for mental relaxation: Bobby.

p. 28 foundational text in mindfulness meditation: Brach.

p. 30 "Put on their own oxygen mask first": Whitney began a yoga and
meditation practice in 2015, and over the last seven years has heard
the "put your own mask on first" reminder many, many times—but
can't remember when she first encountered it, and therefore, whom
to credit for teaching her. It's likely that it was Adriene Mishler,
host of the YouTube channel Yoga with Adriene, or Tara Brach,
but Whitney isn't sure. She thanks them both for the guidance and
insights, regardless.

CHAPTER 2

p. 40 Poe's law was a recurring character in our first book: Phillips and
Milner, *The Ambivalent Internet*.

p. 44 a study of the holes in YouTube's ad policy on hate: Yin and
Sankin.

p. 48 investigation of YouTube's recommendation algorithm: Mozilla
Foundation.

p. 52 assumptions connected to lack of diversity in tech: Phillips and
Milner, *You Are Here*, 49–53.

pp. 52–53 the toxic consequences of the lack of diverse voices in tech: boyd.

pp. 53–55 the reality of the marketplace of ideas: Syed.

pp. 53–55 the history and uses of muted group theory, which describes how members of minority groups are discounted or out-right ignored by authority figures and mainstream institutions: Kramarae.

p. 58 the first article Whitney published where she described the connection between anger and the four *A*s of social media: Phillips, "How to Be Angry on the Internet (Mindfully), Part 1."

p. 58 the liberating and positive potential of anger: Owens.

p. 59 how conversations about "cancel culture" often miss the point and take only certain people's anger seriously: Phillips, "Whose Anger Counts?"

p. 59 how Black people's anger is perceived and responded to (or not) compared to white people's anger: Cooper.

CHAPTER 3

p. 63 where we introduced our stories about redwoods, hurricanes, and the Kansas prairie: Phillips and Milner, *You Are Here.*

p. 64 the power of narrative to persuade and engage with others: Green and Brock. Green and Brock's discussion of narrative transportation, the process by which audiences are transported into narratives, guided how we structured this chapter and framed our narratives.

p. 72 historical overview of the Dust Bowl: "Dust Bowl."

p. 72 something big billows on the horizon behind it: photographic inspiration for this image from "Dust Storm in Morton County, Kansas."

p. 73 the impact of industrial farming on small Kansas towns: McLean.

CHAPTER 4

p. 77 the inspiration for the chapter's opening story: Martin Luther King Jr. The exchange between Jake, Sara, and Principal Smith draws inspiration from Dr. Martin Luther King Jr.'s "Letter from Birmingham Jail." In his letter, King calls out Birmingham's white moderate clergy members. Although the clergy expressed sympathy for the civil rights movement, they had recently released a statement criticizing King's presence in Birmingham and lamenting the civil rights protests for being disruptive, extreme, and untimely. King mused that the protests were indeed unfortunate, but more unfortunate still was the reason the protests were necessary—and where was their lamentation over that? In this way, King's letter exemplifies the harm and violence that can result when civility is valued over justice.

p. 79 where we first developed the biomass model for understanding online offenders: Phillips and Milner, *You Are Here*, 175–177.

p. 90 introduction to concepts of consumable agonies and Black pain: Debra Walker King.

p. 93 discussion of the limitations of facts and fact-checking: Phillips and Milner, *You Are Here*, 149–181.

CHAPTER 5

pp. 104–105 the importance of consent in everyday life: Hancock and MacAree.

pp. 104–105 where we first started exploring consent on social media: Phillips and Milner, *The Ambivalent Internet*.

CHAPTER 6

p. 117 introduction to the concept of the play frame: Bateson.

p. 119 introduction to the concept of "clash-that-makes-sense": Oring. Oring uses the term "appropriate incongruity" to describe the humor response; in this chapter we've translated his phrase into "clash-that-makes-sense."

p. 119 a study of the ambivalence of online humor: Phillips and Milner, *The Ambivalent Internet.*

p. 125 the inspiration for our "Sara and Black-Lady GIFs" story: Jackson.

p. 128 where Whitney first began theorizing zoomed-in humor online: Phillips, *This Is Why We Can't Have Nice Things.*

p. 129 where Ryan first began theorizing internet memes and their ambivalence: Milner.

Bibliography

Bateson, Gregory. "A Theory of Play and Fantasy." In *Steps to an Ecology of Mind*, 177–193. Chicago: University of Chicago Press, 2000. First published 1972 by Chandler (San Francisco).

Bobby, Juna. "Relaxing Your Nervous System." Insight Timer. https://insighttimer.com/meditation-courses/course_relaxing-your-nervous-system.

boyd, danah. "Facing the Great Reckoning Head-On." *Apophenia*, September 15, 2019. https://www.zephoria.org/thoughts/archives/2019/09/15/facing-the-great-reckoning-head-on.html.

Brach, Tara. *True Refuge: Finding Peace and Freedom in Your Own Awakened Heart.* New York: Bantam, 2012.

Bullard, Robert D., and Beverly Hendrix Wright. "The Politics of Pollution: Implications for the Black Community." *Phylon* 47, no. 1 (1986): 71–78.

Buolamwini, Joy. "How I'm Fighting Bias in Algorithms." TED video, March 29, 2017. https://youtu.be/UG_X_7g63rY.

Bushwick, Sophie. "How to Stop Doomscrolling News and Social Media: 'Doomscroll Reminder Lady' Karen K. Ho Explains How to Step Away from the Screen." *Scientific American*, February 12, 2021. https://www.scientificamerican.com/article/how-to-stop-doomscrolling-news-and-social-media/.

Colmer, Jonathan, and Jay Shimshack. "Air Pollution Down in the U.S. but Still Hurts Marginalized Communities Most." *PBS NewsHour*, August 3, 2020. https://www.pbs.org/newshour/health/air-pollution-down-in-the-u-s-but-still-hurts-marginalized-communities-most.

Cooper, Brittney. *Eloquent Rage: A Black Feminist Discovers Her Superpower.* New York: St. Martin's, 2018.

Dhir, Amandeep, Yossiri Yossatorn, Puneet Kaur, and Sufen Chen. "Online Social Media Fatigue and Psychological Wellbeing—a Study of Compulsive Use, Fear of Missing Out, Fatigue, Anxiety and Depression." *International Journal of Information Management* 40 (June 2018): 141–152. https://doi.org/10.1016/j.ijinfomgt.2018.01.012.

"Dust Bowl." Kansas Historical Society. June 2003. https://www.kshs.org/kansapedia/dust-bowl/12040.

"Dust Storm in Morton County, Kansas." Ca. 1935 photo. Kansas Historical Society. https://www.kansasmemory.org/item/211239.

"Exposed: The Scale of Transphobia Online: Exploring Transphobia and Pro-Trans Conversations on Social Media." Brandwatch and Ditch the Label, 2019. https://www.brandwatch.com/reports/transphobia/.

Green, M. C., and T. C. Brock. "The Role of Transportation in the Persuasiveness of Public Narratives." *Journal of Personality and Social Psychology* 79, no. 5 (2000): 701–721. https://doi.org/10.1037/0022-3514.79.5.701.

Grimes, Diane. "How to Be Angry on the Internet (Mindfully), Part 2." *Commonplace*, August 10, 2020. https://commonplace.knowledgefutures.org/pub/p4l9jqut/release/1.

Hancock, Justin, and Fuchsia MacAree. *Can We Talk about Consent? A Book about Freedom, Choices, and Agreement.* London: Francis Lincoln, 2021.

"How Uniontown, Alabama, Became Victim of Environmental Injustice." NowThis News video, October 14, 2017. https://youtu.be/lNik_ZLBsWc.

Islam, A. K. M. Najmul, Samuli Laato, Shamim Talukder, and Erkki Sutinen. "Misinformation Sharing and Social Media Fatigue during COVID-19: An Affordance and Cognitive Load Perspective." *Technological Forecasting and Social Change* 159 (October 2020). https://doi.org/10.1016/j.techfore.2020.120201.

Jackson, Lauren Michele. "We Need to Talk about Digital Blackface in Reaction GIFs." *Teen Vogue*, August 2, 2017. https://www.teenvogue.com/story/digital-blackface-reaction-gifs.

Jha, Amishi. "The Brain Science of Attention and Overwhelm." *Mindful*, November 5, 2020. https://www.mindful.org/youre -overwhelmed-and-its-not-your-fault/.

Kimmerer, Robin Wall. *Braiding Sweetgrass: Indigenous Wisdom, Scientific Knowledge, and the Teachings of Plants*. Minneapolis: Milkweed, 2013.

King, Debra Walker. *African Americans and the Culture of Pain*. Charlottesville: University of Virginia Press, 2008.

King, Martin Luther, Jr. "Letter from Birmingham Jail." August 1963. https://www.csuchico.edu/iege/_assets/documents/susi-letter -from-birmingham-jail.pdf.

Kramarae, Cheris. "Muted Group Theory and Communication: Asking Dangerous Questions." *Women and Language* 28, no. 2 (2005): 55–61.

Lenhart, Amanda, Michele Ybarra, Kathryn Zickuhr, and Myeshia Price-Feeney. "Online Harassment, Digital Abuse, and Cyberstalking in America." Data & Society Research Institute and the Center for Innovative Public Health Research. November 21, 2016. https://datasociety.net/library/online-harassment-digital-abuse -cyberstalking/.

Marwick, Alice, Rachel Kuo, Shanice Jones Cameron, and Moira Weigel. "Critical Disinformation Studies: A Syllabus." Center for Information, Technology, and Public Life, University of North Carolina at Chapel Hill, 2021. https://citap.unc.edu/research /critical-disinfo/.

McLean, Jim. "'Get Big or Get Out' Farming Has Left Kansas Towns Struggling for Survival." KCUR, October 18, 2019. https://www .kcur.org/agriculture/2019-10-18/get-big-or-get-out-farming-has -left-kansas-towns-struggling-for-survival.

Milner, Ryan M. *The World Made Meme: Public Conversations and Participatory Media*. Cambridge, MA: MIT Press, 2016.

Morton, Timothy. *The Ecological Thought*. Cambridge, MA: Harvard University Press, 2012.

Nethery, H. A., IV. "It Is Two Minutes to Midnight: A Plea for Cosmic Pessimism." Omicron Delta Kappa Last Lecture series, Florida Southern College, April 12, 2018.

Notebaert, Karolien. "Unlock Your Wise & Mindful Brain." Insight Timer. https://insighttimer.com/meditation-courses/course_karo lien-notebaert-30-days.

Oring, Elliott. *Jokes and Their Relations*. Lexington: University Press of Kentucky, 1992.

"Overview." Planetary Collective video, 2012. https://vimeo .com/55073825.

Owens, Lama Rod. *Love and Rage: The Path to Liberation through Anger*. Berkeley, CA: North Atlantic, 2020.

Phillips, Whitney. "Whose Anger Counts?" *Boston Review*, August 28, 2020. https://bostonreview.net/articles/whitney-phillips-tk/.

———. "How to Be Angry on the Internet (Mindfully), Part 1." *Commonplace*, August 10, 2020. https://commonplace.knowledge futures.org/pub/95u2fedi/release/1.

———. "To Fight COVID-19, Curb the Spread of Germs—and Rumors." *Wired*, March 11, 2020. https://www.wired.com/story/to-fight -covid-19-curb-the-spread-of-germs-and-rumors/.

———. *This Is Why We Can't Have Nice Things: Mapping the Relationship between Online Trolling and Mainstream Culture*. Cambridge, MA: MIT Press, 2015.

Phillips, Whitney, and Ryan M. Milner. *You Are Here: A Field Guide for Navigating Polarized Speech, Conspiracy Theories, and Our Polluted Media Landscape*. Cambridge, MA: MIT Press, 2021.

———. *The Ambivalent Internet: Mischief, Oddity, and Antagonism Online*. Cambridge, UK: Polity , 2017.

Steenfadt, Olaf. In "Can Platforms Get It Right?" panel discussion at "Disinfo 2020: Prepping the Press" conference, Columbia Journalism School, New York, NY, December 10, 2019.

Syed, Nabiha. "Real Talk about Fake News: Towards a Better Theory for Platform Governance." *Yale Law Journal* 127, October 9, 2017. https://www.yalelawjournal.org/forum/real-talk-about-fake-news.

"Understanding the Stress Response." Harvard Health Publishing, July 6, 2020. https://www.health.harvard.edu/staying-healthy /understanding-the-stress-response.

Vogels, Emily A. "The State of Online Harassment." Pew Research Center, January 13, 2021. https://www.pewresearch.org /internet/2021/01/13/the-state-of-online-harassment/.

Yin, Leon, and Aaron Sankin. "Google Has a Secret Blocklist That Hides YouTube Hate Videos from Advertisers—But It's Full of Holes." *The Markup*, April 8, 2021. https://themarkup.org/google -the-giant/2021/04/08/google-youtube-hate-videos-ad-keywords -blocklist-failures.

"YouTube Regrets: A Crowdsourced Investigation into YouTube's Recommendation Algorithm." Mozilla Foundation, July 2021. https://assets.mofoprod.net/network/documents/Mozilla _You Tube_Regrets_Report.pdf.

Index

influencers
assumptions about the marketplace of ideas and, 54
attention economy and, 44–45
biomass pyramid and, 81
land cultivation metaphor and, 73
information pollution, 4
assumptions about freedom and, 56
awareness of, 8–10
biomass pyramid and, 79
context and, 41
environmental justice and, 5–6
hurricane metaphor and, 70
impact of, 6–7
land cultivation metaphor and, 73, 74
mapping the online environment and, 64
marginalized groups and, 52–53
on-purpose offenders and, 80–82
redwood forest metaphor and, 66
reflecting on, 10–11
story about, 2–3
See also pollution chain reactions
inner circle, 95–96, 123
Instagram
attention economy and, 43
example involving, 87–88
information pollution and, 3–4

J

jokes
context collapse and, 40–41
digitally mediated uh-oh and, 129, 130, 131
gone wrong, stories about 126–127, 132–-133
humor and, 114–115, 124, 125
inside jokes, 118–119
reflection for, 117, 126
snowball effect and, 120
See also online humor and play

R

racism

 anger and, 59

 assumptions and, 52, 54–55

 biomass pyramid and, 79

 digitally mediated uh-oh and, 131

 "Don't feed the trolls" and, 85

 harassment and, 5

 information pollution and, 49–50

 maximizing the energy you give to people who have been harmed and, 88–90

 stories about, 22–23, 77–78, 82–83, 87–88

 white supremacy and, 85

recommendation algorithms, 47–48. *See also* algorithms

Redwood Adventure Park, 1–2, 14–16, 21–24, 127

redwood forest metaphor, 66

 accidental harm and, 101

 bird's-eye-view questions for, 66–67

 first-person-view questions for, 67

 story about, 64–65

 See also hurricane metaphor; land cultivation metaphor

reflection/reflecting

 affordances and, 134

 for communication problems, 34

 ecological thinking and, 10–11, 137

 for handling stress, 29

 hurricane metaphor and, 69, 70

 information pollution and, 8

 for jokes, 117, 126

 for play, 132

 for pollution chain reactions, 21

 redwood forest metaphor and, 67

 reflecting on what energizes you, 90–96

 for sharing memes, 42

 for social media posts, 45

 wellness check-in questions, 27

revenue, 44–45